Twayne's English Authors Series

Sylvia E. Bowman, *Editor*

INDIANA UNIVERSITY

Brendan Behan

 91

Brendan Behan

By TED E. BOYLE

Southern Illinois University

Twayne Publishers, Inc.   ::   New York

PR
6003
.E417
Z6

66884

To the memory of
Professor Robert Dunn Faner

Preface

Brendan Behan's reputation as a writer has seldom been considered, but to such a consideration this book is devoted. In the first chapter I have attempted to demonstrate those influences which shaped Behan's character and his talent, as well as to indicate some of the reasons for Behan's dissipation of his talents. I have not dealt with those aspects of Behan's life not directly related to his writing, for such a consideration remains for Behan's biographer. Chapter 2 is an attempt to place Behan's comic genius in perspective. In chapters 3–6, I have analyzed Behan's major works, hoping to indicate that Brendan Behan, one of the most accomplished drinkers of the twentieth century, was also one of its most accomplished writers. Many people claim to have known Behan well; few of these people know his work at all. The work is as fascinating as the man, and I have quoted extensively from Behan in an attempt to communicate something of the style and flavor of his genius.

I wish here to acknowledge the help of my wife Mary, who typed the manuscript of this book. I also wish to express my thanks to Alan Cohn, and Ralph Bushee of the Southern Illinois University Libraries. Special thanks also to Jimmy Bourke, a scholar and a gentleman, who helped me considerably with the chapter on Behan's life.

TED E. BOYLE

Southern Illinois University
Carbondale

Acknowledgments

I wish gratefully to acknowledge the following publishers for permission to quote from the works indicated:

Little, Brown and Co. for quotations from *Hold Your Hour and Have Another;* Doubleday and Company, Inc., for quotations from *The Scarperer;* Leslie Frewin for quotations from *My Brother Brendan* by Dominic Behan; Bernard Geis Associates for quotations from *Brendan Behan's Island, Brendan Behan's New York,* and *Confessions of an Irish Rebel;* Grove Press, Inc., for the quotations from *The Quare Fellow* and *The Hostage;* Hutchinson and Co., Ltd., for quotations from *The Scarperer, Borstal Boy, Brendan Behan, Man and Showman,* by Rae Jeffs, *Confessions of an Irish Rebel, Hold Your Hour and Have Another; Brendan Behan's Island,* and *Brendan Behan's New York;* Alfred Knopf, Inc., for quotations from *Borstal Boy;* Methuen and Co., Ltd., for quotations from *The Hostage* and *The Quare Fellow;* The New English Library, Ltd., for quotations from *The World of Brendan Behan,* ed. Sean McCann; Routledge and Kegan Paul, Ltd., for quotations from *Beckett and Behan and a Theatre in Dublin,* by Alan Simpson; Twayne Publishers, Inc., for quotations from *The World of Brendan Behan,* ed. Sean McCann; The World Publishing Co., Inc., for quotations from *Brendan Behan, Man and Showman,* by Rae Jeffs; and Simon and Schuster, Inc., for *My Brother Brendan,* by Dominic Behan.

Contents

Contents

Chronology

1923   Brendan Behan born February 9 in Dublin, the first child of Stephen and Kathleen (Kearney) Behan. Mrs. Behan had been married before to Jack Furlong, who left her a young widow with two sons, Rory and Sean, the latter a favorite of Brendan's.

1928– Attended the school of the French Sisters of Charity in
1934   Dublin.

1934– Attended the Christian Brothers School, Dublin.
1937

1937   Attended Day Apprentice School to learn the trade of house painting.

1937   Joined the Irish Republican Army (I.R.A.), transferring from Fianna Éireann, which he had joined in 1931.

1939   Arrested in Liverpool and sentenced to three years' Borstal treatment (the English equivalent of reform school) for illegal I.R.A. activity.

1941   Released from Hollesley Bay, Borstal school; deported to Ireland under an Expulsion Order.

1942   Arrested following row at Glasnevin Cemetery; sentenced to fourteen years for shooting at a policeman. "I Become a Borstal Boy" published in the June, 1942, issue of *The Bell.*

1946   Sentence commuted; released from prison.

1946– House painter and apprentice writer.
1954

1953   *The Scarperer,* by "Emmet Street" published serially in the *Irish Times.*

1954– Weekly column published in the *Irish Press.*
1956

1954   *The Quare Fellow,* Alan Simpson director, opened at the Pike Theatre, Dublin.

1955 Married Beatrice ffrench-Salkeld, daughter of the noted Irish artist.

1956 *The Quare Fellow,* Joan Littlewood director, opened at the Theatre Royal, Stratford, East London.

1958 *An Giall,* the Irish language version of *The Hostage,* opened at Damer Hall, Dublin. *The Hostage,* Joan Littlewood director, opened at the Theatre Royal, Stratford, East London. *The Quare Fellow,* José Quintero director, opened off-Broadway, New York City. *Borstal Boy* published.

1959 *The Hostage* represented Great Britain at the *Théâtre des Nations* festival in Paris. *The Hostage* moved to Wyndham's Theatre in the West End of London.

1960 *The Hostage* opened in New York at the Cort Theatre.

1961 The film version of *The Quare Fellow* opened in London.

1962 *The Hostage* produced off-Broadway, New York City. *Brendan Behan's Island* published.

1963 *Hold Your Hour and Have Another* published. Blanaid Orla Jacqueline Mairead Behan born.

1964 March 20, 1964, Brendan Behan died in Meath Hospital, Dublin. *The Scarperer* published in book form. *Brendan Behan's New York* published.

1965 *Confessions of an Irish Rebel* published.

CHAPTER 1

Life and Influences

> If I am anything at all, I am a man of letters. I'm a writer, a word
> which does not exactly mean anything in either the English, Irish, or
> American language. But I have never seen myself as anything else. . . .
> —Brendan Behan, *Confessions of an Irish Rebel*

WHEN Brendan Behan died on March 20, 1964, in Dublin's
Meath Hospital, Behan the writer had been completely
overshadowed by Behan the brawling drunkard. His reputation
was much like that of the dog whose master had taught him to
play checkers: the dog did not win many games, but the fact that
he could play at all was amazing. When Behan died, people generally did not remark about the passing of a great writer but
about the death of a famous drunk who also wrote a bit. Although
he had created some first-rate literature—*The Quare Fellow, The
Hostage, Borstal Boy*—Behan, through his marathon boozing and
various poses as a rebel, had encouraged the notion that he was a
sort of latter-day but drunker Robert Burns—an unlettered, un-
sophisticated voluptuary who dashed off wee bits of literature in
the brief intervals between glasses of booze.

Behan, however, was a serious writer, a good writer with much
potential to be a great one. That he did not achieve greatness was,
of course, his own fault. He killed himself before he had an opportunity to really test his talents. According to his death certificate,
he died of fatty degeneration of the liver, yet the cause of death
might well have been listed as suicide, for Behan's manner of dying was only nominally different from Hemingway's or Van
Gogh's.

The enormous crowd that gathered at Behan's funeral was,
Dominic Behan insists, paying its respects to the memory of a
kind and generous man, not to a drunkard:

Brendan's funeral (what a strange sound that has) lacked one ingredient—the essential Behan. Or, he was at it right enough, but strangely silent. Probably because there was no one there able to see the funny side of the affair, they were upset and he was sad to see them so, and he was unable to do anything to cheer them up. Maybe they all had their private memories, like the time he went into a hock shop to pawn his typewriter and then handed the money to a poor woman trying to get money for a meal on a bundle of rags. Or when he marched twelve frozen Dubliners into a tailor's one Christmas and ordered one dozen overcoats. The countless people he had saved from being evicted by paying their arrears of rent. They might have come just because they remembered a man who walked into their lives, bought a round of drinks, sang a song or two, and left them with hope. Why they came doesn't really matter, but I'm sure of one thing, they didn't attend his funeral to pay respects to a "brain hit by a bottle." [1]

Another account of Behan's funeral, this one by Rae Jeffs, also emphasizes the breadth of Behan's acquaintance and sympathies:

If Brendan had not been a hero in life, the same was not true at his death. All the colour and drama associated with his name attended his funeral as thousands lined the streets and pavements from Donnybrook to Glasnevin, stopping traffic while the I.R.A., this time aided by a posse of policemen on motorbikes, eased the cortege on its way. In death as in life he had been able to attract all sections of society, for along with President de Valera's delegate, the Tanaiste and members of both Houses of the Oireachtas, who were prepared to overlook the illegality of the I.R.A. on so solemn an occasion, came the titled, the untitled, the famous, the not-so-famous, the unknown, the down-and-outs, and the man on the street whose day perhaps it was the most of all. While Brendan would have loved the marvellous theatre of the spectacle, he would have enjoyed particularly the sight of the old ladies with their shopping baskets standing by the graveside, the children squabbling amongst themselves for a better position, the gravedigger waving his spade in the air to make sure that his one chance of appearing on television did not go unobserved by his friends, and a colleague speaking over his grave in sonorous tones of the privilege of being interred in the Curragh camp with Brendan. At once, the verbal slip echoed in our minds with Brendan's unheard laughter. [2]

Both of these excellent descriptive accounts of Dublin's paying its respects to a famous son only serve to emphasize that the non-literary aspects of Behan's life, and death, always tend to overshadow Behan's writing talent. He was certainly a sensational character, a publicity agent's delight and a hack journalist's dream; but any except the most cursory examination of Behan's work indicates that the man could indeed write, and write well.

That Behan became famous either as a writer or a drinker must certainly be one index of the man's tremendous drive and talent. He was born in Dublin,[3] February 9, 1923, to a family too poor to give him more than the most minimal formal education. From 1928 until 1934 he attended the School of the French Sisters of Charity where he became especially fond of Sister Monica, who was one of the first to recognize Brendan Behan as something different from the common run of Dublin slum ruffians. In fact, Sister Monica was so impressed by young Brendan's intelligence that she informed Behan's mother that the child was a genius. After leaving the French Sisters in 1934, Behan spent three years with the Christian Brothers before learning the house-painting trade at Day Apprentice School.

Behan's formal education, then, was limited, but his active and fertile mind could not be restricted by the accident of his birth into a poor family. During his years in prison, and later, after his release, he was a voracious reader; and largely on his own he gained an encyclopedic knowledge of Irish history and of English and Irish literature. He also taught himself Irish so that he could read Gaelic literature; Behan's Gaelic was so good, in fact, that he first wrote *The Hostage* (*An Giall*) in Irish. He also wrote poetry in Irish, poetry which was good enough to be included in *Nuabhéarsaíocht*, a collection of the best Irish verse written between 1900 and 1950.[4] Behan's spoken Irish may not have been as pure as that which he wrote,[5] yet the fact that he could handle the language at all was exceptional for a man of his background.

Brendan Behan was one of seven children reared in the intensely nationalistic household of Stephen and Kathleen Behan. Rory and Sean were born to Kathleen Kearney from her two years of marriage to Jack Furlong, an Irish patriot who, though involved in the 1916 uprising, died not in the streets of Dublin from an English bullet but in his own bed from pneumonia. Brendan, Seamus, Brian, Carmel, and Dominic, in that order, were the children of Stephen and Kathleen. Indoctrination in Irish nationalism and Irish history and interest generally in things literary were much a part of the Behan household. In *The Hostage* and *Borstal*

Boy Behan drew upon this nationalistic fervor. The day-to-day domestic relationship between Stephen and Kathleen Behan also stimulated Behan's pen. "Moving Out" and "A Garden Party" [6] are lightly satiric one-act plays that deal generally with the eternal but loving conflict between Stephen and Kathleen, and specifically with the move which the Behan family made in 1937 from 14 Russell Street to 70 Kildare Road, Crumlin.

As important as the home atmosphere for the development of Behan the writer was the family's connection with the Queen's Theatre and its lessee, Behan's uncle, P. J. Bourke. Behan, from early childhood until his imprisonment in 1939, regularly attended his uncle's theater, the "poor man's Abbey." Here he became familiar with the music-hall comedies and Dion Boucicault dramas which were a regular feature of the Queen's Theatre program. Later, especially in *The Hostage,* Behan was to draw upon this knowledge for his own writing.

One day before his seventeenth birthday Behan was sentenced to three years of Borstal treatment for his part in the I.R.A. bombing campaign. After being released from the Borstal institution in 1941,[7] Behan took part in a row at Glasnevin Cemetery on Easter Sunday, 1942, and was soon arrested again and sentenced to fourteen years. He was sent to Mountjoy Prison, from which he was successively transferred to two other Irish prisons, Arbour Hill and the Curragh. In the general amnesty of 1946 Behan was released; and, though he was to spend a good many more nights in jail before he died, he never again served a long stretch in prison.

After his second long prison term, Behan began that Dublin-based nomadic existence which was to be his until his death. From 1946 until he achieved world fame in 1956 with the London opening of *The Quare Fellow,* Behan traveled throughout Ireland, England, and France. He followed his trade of house painting, doped racing greyhounds, pimped in Paris, and finally and perhaps most respectably was a free-lance writer for various newspapers—the *Irish Times,* the *Irish Press,* the *People,* and the *Sunday Dispatch.* His most steady employment during this period was a 1954–56 stint with the *Irish Press,* for which he wrote a weekly column and from which was distilled one of his most entertaining books, *Hold Your Hour and Have Another.*

He also did considerable and fairly steady work as a broadcaster for Radio Éireann, doing programs for the national radio in April, 1951 ("Talk About the North Side of Dublin"), and December, 1951 ("Paris Follies"). He also did a series of ten programs from February to July in 1952 ("The Ballad Maker's Saturday Night"), for which he sang ballads and wrote scripts. He did two additional programs under the general title of "Balladmakers' Saturday Night" in 1956, and he also read his excellent short-short story, "A Coat for Confirmation," in 1953. In fact, Behan bid fair to become a permanent fixture on Radio Éireann; for "Moving Out" and "A Garden Party," which were broadcast as occasional pieces in 1952, were intended by Micheal O'hAodha, Productions Director of Radio Éireann, to be part of a radio family serial.

The Quare Fellow was first presented in 1954 at the Pike Theatre in Dublin, but Behan did not achieve real fame until 1956 when *The Quare Fellow* was presented in London. Nineteen fifty-six was also the year of Behan's famous drunken performance on British Broadcasting Company Television, and from this year until his death Behan was to be constantly in the public eye. In October, 1958, *The Hostage* opened at the Theatre Royal in Stratford, East London; in the same month *Borstal Boy* was published. *Brendan Behan's Island,* published in 1959, consists of tape recordings he made with Mrs. Rae Jeffs, plus several short pieces which he had previously published. *Hold Your Hour and Have Another* (1963) is a collection of forty-six of the best columns which Behan had written for the *Irish Press* from 1954 to 1956. *Brendan Behan's New York* (1964) and *Confessions of an Irish Rebel* (1965) were transcribed by Rae Jeffs from tapes which Behan had made shortly before his death. *The Scarperer* (1964) is the book form of a novel which Behan had first published serially in 1953 in the *Irish Times.*

In 1955 Behan was married to Beatrice ffrench-Salkeld. Brendan and Beatrice first met shortly after his release from Borstal, and Brendan was so impressed by her that he called her a "bourgeois swine." [8] In 1954 Beatrice and Brendan renewed the friendship which had started so inauspiciously. When Beatrice and her father were taking a vacation in the Aran Islands, they met Behan with whom they spent "a lovely evening drinking and talking and laughing." [9] Back in Dublin, Beatrice and Brendan saw each other fairly regularly. They attended the opening of *The Quare Fellow* together in December, 1954, and were married in February, 1955, at the Donnybrook Catholic Church. Behan did not tell his family about his wedding, which was at seven in the morning, until the evening of the same day. He told Beatrice that he was afraid his family would think he had betrayed them in that the Behans were of distinctly proletarian stock, and the ffrench-Salkelds were just as distinctly upper class.

Which family was betrayed counted for little, however, and the first few years after Behan's marriage seem to have been among his happiest. After 1960 the times of happiness were few, but before this time two periods of peace and productivity are notable. At the beginning of 1958 the Behans were off to Ibiza, an island off the Spanish coast near the Gulf of Valencia. During the few months here Behan began a novel, *"the catacombs,"* and had completed at least thirty pages of it when he and Beatrice returned to Ireland in March. Beatrice's description of the time spent on Ibiza is idyllic: "Our villa cost seven pounds a month. It had a black-and-white-tiled floor, a balcony with a heart-stopping view of the fields and the sea. The kitchen stove was a tiled charcoal pit. I did the task of cooking in terra-cotta pots. Our water came from a well with a bucket. Brendan walked the beach by day and wrote at night by paraffin lamp. Oh, it was lovely living." [10]

In August, 1958, the Behans went to Sweden at the invitation of Olaf Lagerlöf; and at Ljustero, near Stockholm, Behan corrected the proofs of *Borstal Boy* and also began the translation of *An Giall* into its English version, *The Hostage*. Certainly Beatrice Behan was responsible for creating the sort of atmosphere in which Behan could work in those relatively happy days of 1958. After Sweden, however, Behan was unable to isolate himself sufficiently to get his work done. Rae Jeffs writes perceptively about the time shortly after Behan and Beatrice returned from Sweden: "As his bolt of resistance was tackled by every conceivable type of spanner, his capacity for living, coupled with a real fear of loneliness, would not allow him to resist for long the constant invitations to the feast. His ability to shut himself away to write now began to diminish as success grew, and the unfinished translation of *The Hostage* did not appeal as much as the pub or the binges that brought the newspaper headlines. . . . Brendan had known too much poverty not to be dazzled by the gold dangling in front of his eyes and now he began to boast of the money he was spending each day on drink." [11]

After 1958, Behan became increasingly more erratic in his behavior, and his wife and friends found him nearly impossible to control. He was still able to display himself occasionally for the amusements of the audiences who attended his plays, but he was apparently panicked by having to remain in one place long enough to take honest stock of himself. In March, 1959, Behan traveled to Berlin for the opening of the German production of *The Quare Fellow*. In April, he was in Paris for the *Theâtre des Nations* festival in which *The Hostage*, ironically enough, represented Great Britain. On July 11, 1959, *The Hostage* opened at Wyndham's Theatre in London's West End.

This was the second London run for *The Hostage*, and Behan was not present for the opening. He was having too much fun drinking and enjoying his new fame in Ireland. His celebrations put him in the hospital, but early in the run of *The Hostage* he discharged himself from the hospital and flew to London where he gave one of the most sensational of his drunken performances, insulting audiences and actors alike. The papers, unfortunately, did not chastise Behan; and he was to give many more of these sad performances in the years to come under the impression that he was reflecting glory upon himself and his plays.

In March, 1960, Behan was in London for the opening of his brother Dominic's play *Posterity Be Damned*. Behan was not in good shape when he arrived in London, and excessive drinking after his arrival put him in the hospital again. Out of the English hospital and back in Dublin, Behan tried manfully to stop drinking. Significantly enough, one of the devices he employed was to stay away from Dublin and the pubs where temptation would be too much for him. In September, Behan traveled to New York for the opening of *The Hostage*. He had been on the wagon for six months, and was determined to stay so. He did not; but, except for the notable evening when he became drunk and indulged himself in another of his ridiculous drunken curtain calls, he made a noble effort. In December, 1960, Behan returned to Dublin, determined to resume his work. He failed, began drinking again, and did not stop until he died.

In early 1961 he was again in the United States. Almost frantically he ran about the United States and Canada. In Toronto, where he was to act as master of ceremonies for a jazz review named *Impulse*, Behan was involved in a row with a hotel manager who would not supply him with a bottle of whiskey. Behan spent the night in jail; and, after being released, he promptly got in another brawl and the jazz review folded. Back in New York, Behan "sat cross-legged in the lobby of a staid midtown hotel on a Saturday night, and throwing back his head, warbled a lugubrious Irish ballad called 'I Met My Love in an Irish Grave-Yard.' Astonished guests—men in dinner clothes, women in formal gowns—gathered around him. The flustered management first called the police; then, learning Behan's identity, they cancelled the call and summoned a doctor who took one look at Brendan and called an ambulance." [12]

From coast to coast in both the United States and Canada, Behan continued his stupid behavior, returning to Dublin in July, 1961, a sick half-man. Even the ever patient Beatrice was beginning to turn from her husband and was forced to move out of the house for days at a time when Behan was on a binge. During this time, Behan's friends were desperately attempting to help him, and hopes were high when Behan went to London in October to undergo treatment for alcoholism. David Astor of the *Observer* and Rae Jeffs had arranged for a quiet rest cure in a London nursing home, but once in London Behan foolishly rejected the arrangements of his friends, and decided to return to Dublin.

February, 1962, found Behan in New York for a revival of *The Hostage;* and, though he returned to Dublin in March, the time in New York only undermined his already failing health. In September, he was in England for the *Yorkshire Post*'s literary luncheon held for the authors published by Hutchison. During this trip he also did a television interview for Colin MacInnes, who had written a critical article claiming greatness for Behan's writing. [13] The strain of the party and the television interview proved too much for Behan; and, though he remained relatively sober for both his appearances, shortly after the latter one he embarked on another binge which ended only when he was taken to Westminster Hospital.

Behan walked out of the hospital before he had much of a chance to recuperate; and shortly after, in one of the strangest episodes of his exceptional life, he ended up in a sanitarium for alcoholics. Quite by accident, in a search for a drink at the house of a friend, Behan lurched into the house next door, which was a nursing home for alcoholics. After cajoling by Rae Jeffs, Behan stayed in the sanitarium and allowed himself to be treated; but, in spite of the best efforts of his doctors, his wife, Mrs. Jeffs, and other friends, the cure failed even though he did not drink for a time after leaving the nursing home. Again his fear of remaining in one place too long and of having to look at himself with a clear and objective eye made him nervous, and he decided to go to the south of France for a time. Here he began drinking again, and he returned to Dublin in November, 1962, sick and exhausted. During the next few months he apparently had some relatively sober days, but the sad party that was to end his life continued largely unimpeded by any effort of will on Behan's part.

After a few months in Dublin he became restless and was impelled to run away from himself again. At the end of February, 1963, he flew across the Atlantic to his beloved New York. He had no reason to do so. The days of his triumph on Broadway were long past, but apparently he craved attention as desperately as he did drink. In his sick mind he associated New York with the days of his creative power, with fame, with money; and he felt that transferring his addled mind and ruined body from Dublin to New York would turn the trick—would transform him into the Brendan Behan he used to be. This last trip to New York represented Behan's last desperate clutching at life from the depths of the death-in-life he had molded for himself. A year and a few days after his last arrival in New York, Behan would be dead.

Only two or three very short periods of useful human activity were to be left to Behan during the last year of his life. In April, 1963, he and Rae Jeffs taped the largest part of *Confessions of an Irish Rebel* in New York, she having made the journey from England for this express purpose. Mrs. Jeffs left New York before the taping of *Confessions* was finished, but she returned at the end of May at which time, by working around Behan's alcoholic collapses, the tapes were completed. Behan finally became so ill, however, that his wife and Mrs. Jeffs decided it was imperative to get him home again. After a stopoff in London, Behan was back in Dublin in July; and from this time until his death he was almost constantly in and out of hospitals. Remarkably, however, in November of 1963, Behan pulled himself together sufficiently to tape *Brendan Behan's New York*, but the respite was short. From the end of November, 1963 (Behan used John Kennedy's assassination as an excuse to start his binge), until his death in March, 1964, Behan was either dead drunk, relatively drunk, or in a diabetic coma. Even the birth of his daughter on November 23, 1963, failed to impede his sad, slow suicide. On March 20, 1964, Brendan Behan died.

Had Behan possessed a weak constitution, he would have died in 1959 when he had his first serious breakdown. In fact, the last five years of Behan's existence cannot accurately be called "life." He was an extremely sick man; and, ironically enough, the amazing strength and resiliency of his constitution were a curse rather than a blessing. If his assorted ailments had been sufficient to disable him long enough for the doctors and psychiatrists to do their work, Behan might have lived much longer. It is indeed tempting to wish that Behan had possessed more self-control, that he had lived longer and written more. But such wishful thinking tends to ignore the fact that the exuberance of Behan's genius was a function of his magnificent lack of self-control; that had he been able to stop drinking, his creative capacity would probably have dried up as well.

This is not to say that Behan had to be drunk to write. It is to say that had he achieved enough peace of mind to stop drinking, he would also have lost that restiveness, that basic dissatisfaction with the way the world is, which seems to be one of the major stimulations for the twentieth-century writer. Speculation regarding what Behan might have done also tends to obscure the fact that Behan wrote two plays which have become classics of the contemporary theater, one of the best autobiographies ever written, and a series of excellent short pieces. In fact, one might say that he never wrote anything bad; for most of the obviously inferior material which was published under Behan's name was the product of his last sad years when he was speaking into the tape recorder what he no longer had the capability or courage to scratch out on a blank piece of paper.

But one does not criticize the efforts of Mrs. Rae Jeffs who helped Behan tape record *Brendan Behan's Island, Brendan Behan's New York,* and *Confessions of an Irish Rebel.* Behan would have done nothing during his last six years without Mrs. Jeffs's prodding. And the possibility always existed that he might, at any time, have been able to assume the burden of writing without the aid of a literary midwife. Behan never assumed this burden, of course, though it is clear that Mrs. Jeffs wanted him to. It is also clear that in all dealings with Behan, she was motivated only by a sincere and studied admiration for Behan's genius.

I *Behan's Insecurity*

The writer in the twentieth century must, above all, take himself seriously, even if he must crouch shivering behind the tradition of the English Catholic Church, as did T. S. Eliot; make up his own theory of history and esthetics, as did William Butler Yeats; or construct his own language, as did James Joyce. Behan, though never giving up his faith, was too honest to use the church as a shield and as a final answer, as did Eliot. Though the history of Ireland was unbearably painful for Behan, he refused to ameliorate this pain by retreating to ingeniously farfetched systems of "phases" and "gyres," as did Yeats. And, though Behan despaired that either Gaelic or English could persuade either the Irish or the English to recognize the greatness that Ireland might have claimed, he did not retreat to a language of his own invention as did Joyce in *Finnegans Wake*.

In the elaborate systems of Eliot, Joyce, and Yeats, however, is inherent a quality which Behan never possessed—an overwhelming and egoistic self-confidence. All of these men believed sufficiently in their talents to be able to ignore either the criticism or the adulation of the public; and, if they hid behind religion, history, or esthetics, they seldom doubted the wisdom of doing so. Behan, who was thrown out of more taverns than most people have been in; Behan, who made so many drunken performances on the stage that his audiences began to expect one as a part of his plays; Behan, who seemed to be happiest the more offensive the spectacle he was making of himself, never believed in himself. His uncontrollable desire to be always the center of attention was obviously a direct result of his fear that he was unworthy of being noticed.

Behan's reaction to appearing on television is certainly illustrative of his lack of the presence which a sincere self-confidence would have given him. Rae Jeffs reports how startled she was, having been taken in by the public image of Behan, when she discovered that public attention put a severe strain upon him. Behan had come to Mrs. Jeffs's office seeming rather nervous and extremely ill at ease:

After a while I noticed he was having to stop at regular intervals to brush the sweat off his brow with his right hand, and assuming that he was feeling the effects of the previous evening's bout, I suggested a chaser. To my amazement he refused, became harassed and distracted as he asked me to tell him about the plans for a television interview. I explained that I would collect him from Blackheath the following afternoon to go to Birmingham, the headquarters of A.B.C. Television, and that Kenneth Allsop, the interviewer whom Brendan had met previously, was to travel on the train as well. He met my remarks in morbid silence, becoming increasingly more hangdog in manner and appearance. Suddenly, but not unexpectedly for it was quite in character, his attitude changed, but the reason for it startled me. He made it emphatically clear that he loathed and detested the 'goggle box.' It was my first experience of the anguish he suffered each time he appeared on television, and later I was to learn that, for a man who loved to be in the public eye, the mental and physical strain it imposed on him was extraordinary.[14]

The interview with Allsop was a success in spite of Behan's extreme nervousness. Such was not the case two years earlier, shortly after the London opening of *The Quare Fellow*, when Behan was interviewed on B.B.C. Television by Malcolm Muggeridge. On this occasion, Behan was so drunk that he lapsed into an embarrassing incoherence. Muggeridge was later to consider Behan's performance pleasant and "most rewarding," [15] for Behan doubtless added excitement to the otherwise rather staid B.B.C. programming; and Muggeridge's English audience surely was amused to see its prototypical notion of the drunken Irishman confirmed. To Behan's friends and family, however, the B.B.C. interview was yet another instance of Behan's inability to resolve his self-doubt.

Time and again, those who knew Behan well noted that his drinking was a symptom of his insecurity. In 1947 Behan wrote a one-act play entitled *Gretna Green* for an I.R.A. fund-raising concert in commemoration of two I.R.A. men who were executed for their part in the 1939 bombing campaign. The play, which Behan wrote in only two days, had only three characters who waited and talked outside the jail in which the two I.R.A. men were to be hanged. Behan, apparently because of his enthusiasm for the concert, even agreed to act in the play, and he attended all the rehearsals, giving every indication of carrying out his promise. Yet several hours before the play was to be presented, he decided he would not go on. " 'I'm a writer,' he said without batting an eyelid —'not an actor.' " [16]

Undoubtedly Behan was afraid to act in his own play, afraid of appearing before the audience which he so desperately wanted. The night of the play, Behan showed up drunk, obviously terrified by a sober view of his play and by the audience reaction to it. Behan's behavior was generally the same seven years later when *The Quare Fellow* was first produced. Again, Behan appeared at rehearsals, though this time he was not to be an actor. Again Behan was obviously nervous, as Alan Simpson's account makes clear:

As the momentous day drew nearer, the atmosphere became too much for Brendan and he took solidly to the bottle, appearing at intervals accompanied by some friendly but uncomprehending soak whom he had acquired in his perambulations through the various pubs in the area. The latter, puzzled as to why he had been dragged away from his creamy pint to this strange, cold garage in a back lane, would sit in the auditorium, muttering amiable obscenities, while Brendan dug him in the ribs and repeated again and again, "I wrote that!" The climax was reached at the dress rehearsal, when the author arrived with only sufficient equilibrium to last him to the door of the theatre. He then collapsed in a heap on the floor, and I had to have him lifted on to the back seat, where he reclined, resplendently comitose, for the entire length of the play. The friendly but persistent complaints from the cast that they could not hear each other's lines, made it necessary for me to detail an assistant stage manager to sit beside our pride and hope, and shake him every time his snores rendered the dialogue inaudible.[17]

On the opening night of *The Quare Fellow* Behan's family and friends carefully maintained his alcoholic equilibrium. The object was to keep Behan from, on the one hand, becoming so thirsty as to bolt out of the theater and, on the other, from becoming so drunk as to disrupt the performance. The anesthesia was successfully maintained, and after the show Simpson advised Behan to be circumspect as he addressed the audience after the play. Behan replied, " 'Oh, God, no, I'd be *terrified* [italics mine]. I'll tell you what I'll do. I'll sing a song.' So to a surprised and delighted audience, he gave a good, if alcoholic rendering of Sean O'Casey's 'Red Roses for Me,' which was received with general acclaim." [18]

In the case of both *Gretna Green* and *The Quare Fellow*, Behan's anxieties were obvious, and it was also obvious that his drinking was at least partially accountable to his nervousness and insecurity. One does not deny that Behan immensely enjoyed drinking in and for itself, yet his refusal to act in *Gretna Green* and his admission of his terror of addressing the audience after *The Quare Fellow* suggest an inordinate fear of being in the limelight that he courted. By the time of *The Hostage* and *Borstal Boy*, Behan was more obviously a drunk, less obviously a frightened man, yet his regular drunken curtain calls and his generally offensive behavior were deeply rooted in his insecurity.

For a time, Behan's writing, the love of his wife, and the roar of the crowd were sufficient to convince him that he and his life were worthwhile. During his last three or four years, he was bitter and disappointed with his writing, with his marriage, and with the crowds he could always gather. But his real trouble was that he never really liked or believed in himself. As Alan Brien, in his obituary of Behan in the *Sunday Telegraph*, says, "There was also, (though many may find it hard to believe), a shy, insecure Brendan who was worried and embarrassed by the headlines he could always command. If he was reluctant to write, if he began each new play with the author's curtain speech, this was not through arrogance or vanity. It was because he was deeply suspicious of his own talent, and sought continual reassurance of his abilities. He never believed what we critics wrote about him—but we were right and he was wrong." [19]

II *Critical Misunderstanding*

The fact that Behan's work was never very well understood must have caused him considerable pain and must also have affirmed his suspicions of his deficiencies. Most of what has been written about Behan, either during his own lifetime or since, deals with the real issues of Behan's work only in the most cursory way. Augustine Martin's *Threshold* article on Behan is an excellent case in point, but it must be added that Martin is not any more guilty of distortion than most of the others who have written about Behan. The "quare fellow" who gives Behan's first full-length play its title is, as Behan wrote the script, condemned to death for the murder of his brother; but Martin identifies the "quare fellow's" crime as that of murdering his wife. The hangman in *The Quare Fellow* is a boisterous sort who is very much bothered by taking the life of another human being. As a consequence of the guilt he feels, the hangman can do his job only if he is drunk. To insure that he is not too drunk to perform, the hangman brings a keeper with him to each job. Martin, apparently remembering the hangman's keeper, identifies the hangman as "a cheerful, innocuous little man who sees the execution simply as a job to be done." [20] Martin correctly identifies the effectiveness of the humor in Behan's play, but his failure to correctly identify either the crime of the "quare fellow" or the identity of the hangman must ultimately lead to an inaccurate interpretation. It seems the journalists and critics expected very little of Behan's work, and therefore did not think it worth their while to examine it too closely.

Behan undoubtedly deserved more serious critical attention than he received, but he was not sure enough of his writing to demand such attention. As it was, he drew the gaze of the critics and the public alike away from his work by building a public image which gave the world exactly what it expected from him. He was too gentle and amiable, too weak and unsure, to do otherwise.

The shame is that Behan believed that only sensationalism—in his work and in his life—was required of him. Perhaps, if the critics had required more of him, he would have demanded more of himself. Certainly he would not have been satisfied to remain a house painter, for the audience he would have found as a painter who also sang and told clever stories simply would not have satiated him. He needed a larger audience; and, though he indeed gained it, he gained it perhaps a bit too easily. His talent and his need to be heard were so great that he surely could have raised the quality of his writing to meet the more objective critical standards which should have been applied to his work from the start. However imperceptive the criticism of Behan's work was, it surely acted only as a catalyst. Behan's suicidal insecurity would in any case have eventually killed him and his work.

The stage personality of the Irish drunk which Behan had before used as a tool to call attention to his writing became in the last five or six years of his life his reason for being, his substitute for work. This sensitive, intelligent, and perceptive man, this writer who could make an obscure "quare" fellow universally interesting, was at the last frantically attempting to make his false personality interesting by dropping names which had associated with it. In that sad and almost totally insignificant book, *Brendan Behan's New York*, Behan is forced to fill his pages, or more accurately his tape, with reminiscences of the famous. At a *bar mizvah* service for Leonard Lyons' son, he meets Frank Loesser, Ethel Merman, and Paddy Chayevsky. Tallulah Bankhead tells him a tired joke. In Greenwich Village he meets Allen Ginsberg, Jack Kerouac, Thornton Wilder, and the late James Thurber. Behan simply thought none of his own work worth talking about. He drank more and more to hide this horrible fact from himself, and finally his liver died, his brain and creativity having preceded it by about three years.

Certainly few have had as many reasons to drink as did Brendan Behan. He was indeed a kind and sensitive person; in fact, too sensitive, says brother Brian: "Underneath his ebullience he was a quivering mass of too much feeling. Feelings deep, raw and violent that were liable to explode at the slightest provocation. Then like a mad stallion he couldn't bear to be bridled by anyone." [21] Brendan cared too much for his family, for his church, and for Ireland. His family, because of its poverty and Behan's years in jail could not, unfortunately, equip him with much stability. The church excommunicated him. English cruelty and Irish stupidity destroyed the Ireland he worked for. He cared; he was frustrated; and he attempted to hide this frustration behind enormous waterfalls of booze. He was a romantic, and he laughed and he drank largely because he was sensitive enough to discern the absurdity of his idealistic commitment in a world and nation where the rewards seemed to be greatest for the cynics and the non-committed.

III *Behan's Family*

Brendan Behan could not escape commitment. To describe his family as a hotbed of Irish nationalism would be a description as understated as it is trite. Behan was first seen by his father through prison bars. This time, for Brendan was only two weeks old, the father was on the inside, the son on the outside looking in. Stephen Behan was in Kilmainham Prison—the cellmate of Sean T. O'Kelly, who was later to become President of Ireland—not because he was a criminal, but because he was a patriot. When Brendan Behan became a young man, Stephen Behan could hardly be so hypocritical as to lecture his son for participating in the fight to win full Irish control of the six counties, for earlier Stephen had been involved in the fight to win all thirty-two. Nor could Stephen be shocked at Brendan's going to jail in the name of Irish patriotism, for the son was merely following the example of the father.

In one respect, however, Stephen Behan gave Brendan an excellent example which was certainly not followed. Stephen worked hard and steadily at his trade of painting, and he was nearly always able to climb to the top of his ladder on a Monday morning. In fact, Stephen rose to the top of his trade and was until his death in 1967 the president of the Irish National Painters' and Decorators' Trade Union. His steady and conservative attitude toward his work, however, seemed an anomaly in the mercurial Behan family. In fact, Stephen's attitude toward his work seemed even to be a contradiction of his own personality.

Alan Simpson, in his excellent book on Beckett and Behan, does not describe the conservative aspects of Stephen Behan's character as dominant: "Stephen has always operated on the simple basis of 'If you have it, spend it,' first on necessities such as drink and then, if there is anything left over, on luxuries like food, clothing, and shelter. He shows no observable *bourgeois* 'love' for his family of seven; he holds to no accepted code of behaviour except that of good fellowship." Simpson adds, however, that Stephen is a wonderfully kind man: "Of all the fathers I could have had, were I to be given the choice, I personally would not wish a better than Stephen." [22] Perhaps it was merely age which slowed Stephen down sufficiently to make him a respectable member of the trade community.

Certainly as a youth he was so fiery as to cause some misgiving to the painting contractor looking for a steady, sober employee. Those who lived in the Russell Street tenement which was the early home of the Behan family remember Stephen Behan's temper:

Stephen Behan! I remember when he was let out of prison with all them other IRA men after the treaty. With a big red beard flowing like a demon he dashed up the stairs and caught poor Mr. Costigan in the bed and cried like a lunatic as he lifted him up to smash him on the door. "Are you the dirty bastard that's bein' makin' my wife's life a hell while I've been away?" And with that he flung that young man from the top to the bottom of 14 Russell Street. Poor Mr. Costigan, he's walked with a limp ever since. And him a pipe major in a band.[23]

Stephen Behan, then, was an active Irish patriot, and his advanced years did not weaken his Republican fervor. Stephen still enjoyed the pleasant hours spent in the taverns, and reports still circulate concerning his violent temper. But Stephen Behan always provided for his family, both when it lived in the run-down tenements on Russell Street and later when the family moved to 70 Kildare Road; and it was literally at his father's knee that Brendan was given his first contact with literature. During the long, cold Dublin evenings, between paydays when Stephen did not have sufficient money to go to the pub, the father regularly read to his children. Brendan himself remembered, "During the earlier part of the week my old man would read us Dickens and Shaw and Charles Lever, who wrote *Charles O'Malley* and who was Shaw's first model in writing. They were great gatherings and I sitting at his feet around a big fire, taking it all in. The preface in *John Bull's Other Island* I knew almost by heart, but happily I forgot everything he read from Marcus Aurelius, which put years on me."[24]

Although it is popular to think, with George Wellwarth, that Behan was a "primitive author . . . —instinctive, untutored, uninfluenced,"[25] Behan's father was a very important influence on Behan the man and Behan the writer. In fact, Alan Simpson maintains that, in order to understand Behan or his work, one must know Stephen Behan, the father. Simpson might well have added Behan's mother and grandmother to the list of the people who shaped Behan to such an extent that his life seemed in some measure merely to be extensions of theirs. Stephen Behan read to the children in the evening, and Mrs. Behan, as if not to be outdone, read to the seven children at odd moments during the day, having a book in her hand even while she was at the washtub.[26] Certainly Brendan Behan was also strongly influenced by his mother's nationalistic idealism. The British, in fact, seemingly chose one of the milder and less dangerous Behans when they clapped Brendan into jail; for the British overlooked Brendan's mother, Kathleen. If each Irishman had contributed as much to the cause as did Mrs. Behan, Ireland would have been long since free, united, and probably oppressing the English. "We raised them all to the Cause, we did," [27] says Mrs. Behan; unfortunately Brendan really believed what his mother and father told him about the cause. He was too faithful a son.

The atmosphere in which Brendan Behan was reared is made most evident by a reminiscence of Rae Jeffs. Early in 1960 Mrs. Jeffs, an Englishwoman employed by Hutchison Publishers, was having lunch with Brendan, his wife Beatrice, Mrs. Kathleen Behan, and other relatives. Suddenly Mrs. Behan turned on Rae Jeffs:

I heard Kathleen Behan call across, "You killed Kevin Barry." On looking around the rest of the company I was forced, by the direction of her stare, to acknowledge that she was speaking to me. I hadn't the slightest idea to whom she was referring, but guessed that the remark was provocative because Brendan angrily told his mother to "leave the girl alone. She knows nothing about these things." I felt the storm clouds gather above my head, but in the next breath, Kathleen Behan blew them away by singing the lovely song about Kevin Barry which I now know so well.

> In Mountjoy Jail, one Monday morning,
> High upon the gallows tree,
> Kevin Barry gave his young life
> For the cause of liberty.
> Only a lad of eighteen summers
> Yet no one can deny
> As he walked to death that morning
> He proudly held his head on high . . .[28]

Such behavior, however, is not extraordinary for a woman who claims that at the age of seven she could recite every word of "Who Fears to Speak of '98." Mrs. Behan was such a fervid revolutionary, in fact, that one revolution was not really enough for her. The whole family supported the Spanish Popular Front; and Brendan, again taking his parents too seriously, volunteered for service in Spain. Unfortunately, he was accepted and was sent instructions telling him to report to a ship bound for Spain and the Civil War. Mrs. Behan, however, intercepted the letter and destroyed it,[29] thus assuring that her son would at least not have to face Spanish guns or rot in Spanish prisons.

Even when Behan was at the peak of his fame and of his sick drunkenness, he saw his family regularly. It was his habit, in fact, to dash into his family's house and carry his mother off on a drinking tour of Dublin. Behan loved to be soothed by the presence of his mother, as well as by the numberless pints he consumed in the bars of Dublin.

Certainly Brendan Behan was deeply influenced by his family, by Irish history, by the I.R.A., and by the Catholic Church. When Behan was arrested in Manchester in March, 1947, for breaking the deportation order against him, Eoin O'Mahoney, the Irish genealogist, raconteur, and lawyer, flew to England to defend Behan. The charges against him were serious—he had not only broken the deportation order; he had in his possession at the time of his arrest an identity card of a member of the Royal Air Force —and O'Mahoney must have put up a masterful defense to get Behan off with only three months. In any case, as a part of his defense of Behan, O'Mahoney described Brendan as a "spiritual love child of the Irish Revolution." When the case was reported in the press, however, the word "spiritual" was dropped from O'Mahoney's description of his client. Brendan's mother was scandalized, but Behan himself, even though he at first pretended shock, seemed to prefer the misquotation. The description of Behan as a "love child of the Irish Revolution" is accurate, for Ireland and its revolution made an outcast of Brendan Behan; took him from his family; threw him out of the Catholic Church; and finally, when he attained fame, never fully acknowledged him, but accepted him reluctantly with a snigger and with a prudish sense of outraged Victorianism.

Brendan Behan could not have helped becoming a revolutionary. He probably could not have helped becoming rather self-indulgent as well, for he apparently was the family pet, though Kathleen Behan strongly denies this, putting the blame for Brendan's being spoiled on his paternal grandmother: "She was an oul' fashioned lady, rest her soul. She'd take him to funerals because with his dark curls he was so darling, it cheered everyone up. And at funerals he learned to drink before he was six years old." [30] Mrs.

Behan, protesting too much, it seems, says that her children were "all the same to me, although people think Brendan was a pet of mine, but he wasn't. Da's mother—Stephen's mother—petted him a terrible lot, but I didn't." [31]

James Bourke, Behan's cousin, backs Mrs. Behan's description of young Brendan's relationship with his Granny English: "Christine English certainly influenced Brendan. I don't think she ever left his mind. She owned property in Fitzgibbon Street . . and two houses in Russell Street . . No. 13 and 14 (where Brendan was born). He was her first grandson. She brought him everywhere with her, and into pubs, where she was delighted if an acquaintance mistook her grandson for her own son. He got the taste of porter from her bucket and took his first public drink after a funeral in Gills . . . at the corner of Russell Street." [32] Behan's brother Brian also notes the coddling which the Behan family lavished on Brendan: "He had all the wild wilfulness of my mother, but with no chain to bind him. Spoiled from birth by an overabundance of talk and flattery, he denied himself nothing. People destroy people. To make a God of someone is to destroy them as surely as driving a knife into their back." [33]

IV *Behan and Ireland*

That Brendan Behan was born Irish was a measured blessing. Certainly Irish settings and the peculiarities of the Irish character are very evident in his writing. Yet Behan attained his real recognition in England and in the United States, not in Ireland. Certainly the Irish can offer the simple and ready excuse of poverty when it is asserted that they might have looked upon the early Behan with a bit more interest—after all, the extra money for the purchase of a theater ticket or a book is not present in too many Irish purses. Yet the impression which overwhelms one when he reads of the reception which Behan's work received in Ireland is simply that much of the Irish public and many Irish critics were prudish and jealous where Brendan Behan and his work were concerned. Behan was deeply insulted that his work was so viciously attacked by Irish journalists and critics and that *Borstal Boy* was banned in his homeland. Sean McCann in his perceptive and sympathetic essay on Behan notes that though Behan frequently joked about the criticism which his work received in Ireland, "he was badly hurt. . . . Above all else he wanted recogni-

tion in his own country." [34] Yeats and Joyce had sufficient faith in
themselves to transcend the prudish outrage of the Irish public,
but Behan could never ignore Ireland sufficiently. Behan traveled
to the Continent, to Canada, to both coasts of the United States,
but almost masochistically he always returned to Ireland. He
yearned for Irish approval; he received only a very grudging acceptance. This situation must have helped to convince him that he
lacked enduring literary talent.

V   Behan and the I.R.A.

An unmistakable influence on Brendan Behan, one which calls
for no conjecture at all, was his work in the Irish Republican
Army. Behan was an Irish Rebel "ab ova," becoming formally at-
tached to the cause when he joined Fianna Éireann at the age of
seven; and he remained a member until he was fourteen, at which
time he was transferred to the I.R.A. Brendan Behan's involvement in I.R.A. activities was, however, not what popular opinion
of Behan would recognize. That is, those I.R.A. incidents which
sent Behan to prison and put his name in the newspapers even
before he caused his sensation as a playwright seem in retrospect
to be accidents caused by Behan's drunken juvenile delinquence.
The arrest in Liverpool, the foolhardy trip to England to help
Dick Timmons escape, and above all the incident at Glasnevin
cemetery, tell one little about Behan's sympathy for the Republican cause. Certainly Behan felt most strongly that Ireland should
be completely free from English control. Yet the incidents for
which he was arrested seem motivated more by a wish to call
attention to Brendan Behan than any deeply felt desire to save
Ireland from British oppression. Any objective examination of the
more notorious events in Behan's I.R.A. career leads unmistak-
ably to this conclusion.

In January, 1939, the I.R.A. addressed an ultimatum to the British, the terms of which Sean O'Callaghan reproduces in his history
of the I.R.A.:

I have the honour to inform you that the Government of the Irish
Republic, having as its first duty towards the people, the establishment
and maintenance of peace and order, herewith demand the withdrawal
of all British Armed Forces stationed in Ireland. These forces are an
active incitement to turmoil and civil strife, not only in being a symbol
of hostile occupation, but in their effect and potentialities as an invad-

ing army. It is essentially the duty of the Government to establish relations of friendship between the Irish and all other peoples. We must insist on the withdrawal of all British Forces from our country, and a declaration from your Government renouncing all claims to interfere in our domestic policy. We shall regret if this fundamental feeling is ignored, and be compelled to intervene actively in the military and commercial life of your country, as your Government are now intervening in ours. The Government, in the behalf of the public, believe that a period of four days is sufficient for your Government to signify its intention in the matter of the military evacuation and for the issue of your declaration in respect of our country. Our populace has the right of appropriate action without further notice, if, at the expiration of this period of grace, these conditions remain unfulfilled.

> Signed: STEPHEN HAYES
> PEADAR O'FLAHERTY
> LAURENCE GROGAN
> PATRICK FLEMING
> GEORGE PLUNKETT
> SEAN RUSSELL [35]

To punish the English for not complying with the eviction notice, the I.R.A. launched a campaign of terror in English cities. The campaign in general, and Behan's part in it in particular, were characterized by ineffectuality. The only fact which rendered the campaign anything but totally harmless was the occasional brutality which occurred—brutality, it must be added, which was more the result of accident than intent.

Fifteen-year-old Brendan Behan attended I.R.A. training school for sabotage activities in 1938. In early 1939 he was arrested in Liverpool and the arresting officers had little trouble proving Behan's apprehension justified. In young Behan's possession were found a quantity of gelignite and ingredients used in making the I.R.A.'s favorite sort of homemade bomb. Behan's "Sinn Fein conjurors outfit," as he was to call it in *Borstal Boy*, contained a number of toy balloons plus a supply of potassium chlorate, sugar, and sulfuric acid. Behan had learned in his I.R.A. training school how to inject a small quantity of sulfuric acid into a balloon, allowing the acid to eat slowly through the balloon and come into contact with the sugar-potassium chlorate mixture, thus causing an incendiary explosion.

Behan, when he returned to Ireland, many times indicated that his mission was to blow up the British battleship "King George

V." Blowing up the battleship was, of course, a clear impossibility; but Behan's mission in general seems to have been very foggily thought out. He had little notion of what he was to do with his kit of explosives when he got to England, and his trip, all who knew Behan agree, was an independent effort. Finally, Behan's mission to Liverpool seems more motivated by his wanting to call attention to himself than by his loyalty to the Republican cause. The I.R.A. only offered Behan an excuse; without the I.R.A. he would have found some other way to indulge his need for adventure and his desire to be noticed.

In any case, there can be little doubt that Brendan Behan did not fully realize the seriousness of the mission which he undertook. Reared in surroundings where violence and hatred of the British were a way of life, Behan's English trip takes on the character of an irrational juvenile prank. Behan was not a dangerous saboteur and murderer, and no solid record exists of his having been concerned in any of the more desperate I.R.A. activities. Certainly, he broke a few heads and lost a few teeth defending the cause in barroom brawls; certainly, he was a member in full standing of the I.R.A.; it is extremely doubtful, however, that Brendan Behan ever took a human life in the name of the I.R.A.

A candid remark which Behan himself made about his participation describes his role fairly well: "I'm not a warlike man—as a matter of fact a highly ineffectual one. The I.R.A. had sufficient good military sense never to make me more than a messenger boy." [36] Behan was not always so candid. When he realized that money was to be made by not correcting those who described him as a fearless and dangerous rebel, the true Brendan Behan, idealistic but ineffectual with anything but words, became obscured.

Had Brendan Behan been bent upon homicide, he certainly had sufficient chances to satisfy his lust both inside and outside prison walls. When Behan was arrested in Liverpool, he had no gun, but certainly he could have made things harder for the arresting officers than he did. Characteristically, as he reports his arrest, Behan apologizes for not putting up a better fight. But he also seems to realize that he was not really a very desperate character. In his account of his arrest in Liverpool, Behan writes with a gentle irony:

"Got a gun, Paddy?" asked the sergeant.

"If I had a gun you wouldn't have come through that door so shag-
ging easy."

He looked at me and sighed, as if I had said nothing, or as if he had
not heard me.[37]

Examination of the details of the events surrounding Behan's
trouble at Glasnevin cemetery indicates that the factors motivat-
ing him in this brawl were closely parallel to those involving him
in the I.R.A. bombing campaign. At Glasnevin, as in his inefficient
attempts at terrorism, Behan seems to have been overwhelmed by
the desire of the moment to thrust himself to the center of the
stage. Behan's own account in *Confessions of an Irish Rebel* un-
derlines the spontaneous nature of the Glasnevin disturbance. On
the way to the cemetery Behan had fallen in with a young brick-
layer named Cafferty. They had noticed that three I.R.A. officers
were being stalked by the police. On the way back from the cemetery the police moved in for the arrest:

Everyone was shouting and saying things and one big ugly-faced
policeman going mad with the temper and shouting himself to tell
them to shut up, when all of a sudden somebody screamed, "That man
has a gun," and I looked round and saw the steel glint of a revolver in
one I.R.A. officer's hand and he was altogether hysterical.

"I'll use it, I'll use it," he screamed.

Christ, said I in my own mind, why wasn't I back in Borstal or
Feltham Boys' Prison, in solitary? At least I would be there in peace
and on my own instead of here with my guts twisted up inside me.

As I snatched the revolver out of the officer's hand the police opened
fire. I didn't, and not until they opened fire did I fire back at them and,
still firing, Cafferty and I made a desperate run for it.[38]

Behan's part in the Glasnevin incident was clearly impulsive, obviously stupidly egotistic, and probably the result of his being
drunk at the time. This assertion is substantiated by the eyewit-
ness account of Andrew Nathan, one of the I.R.A. men Behan
mentions in his story about the shooting incident at Glasnevin.
The story which Nathan told to Anthony Butler differs only
slightly from Behan's, yet several details which Nathan mentions,
and Behan does not, emphasize the fact that Behan was drunk at
Glasnevin:

The shooting did not take place at the cemetery but at De Courcy Square, which is a considerable distance from the main gates. The parade had dispersed and as Andrew Nathan, Lazarian Mangan and Joseph Buckley walked alone side by side they were approached by members of the Special Branch, the police section which kept an eye on the I.R.A. Detectives Martin Hanrahan and Patrick Kirwin caught Mr. Nathan by his arms and held him while Lazarian Mangan drew his gun and ran out to the centre of the road where he hesitated for a moment. Brendan Behan who had not been with any of those initially involved came up and called to Mangan: "Use it! Use it!"

Mangan still hesitated and Brendan with a significant gesture threw off his coat and jacket and shouted: "Give it to me and I'll shoot the bastards!" Mr. Nathan can still vividly recall the money and odds and ends rolling around the road from Brendan's discarded clothing.

Firing two shots at a range of about fourteen yards—the width of an average street—Brendan then ran further ahead before turning and firing again. He then ran away as other police closed in.[39]

Newspaper reports prove the correctness of Nathan's account, and it is interesting to note that he does not report that the police fired at all, even though Behan vehemently insisted they had fired first. Surely, if the police had fired, they probably would not have missed at a range of only fourteen yards. As for Behan, it is apparent he did not really intend to shoot anyone. Clearly, he was interested only in the fireworks, only in celebrating Irish Republicanism by shooting off a couple of skyrockets. Just as clearly, Behan was drunk. Why, says Anthony Butler, would a man fling off both his overcoat and his jacket, except as a grand drunken show? "It is the typical gesture of an intoxicated man in a condition of intense emotional excitement. In this light, Brendan's intervention was hardly one for which he could be held responsible." [40] But Behan was held responsible, cruelly so; for shooting at the policemen in De Courcey Square, Behan received a sentence of fourteen years. He did not serve even half the sentence, for, entering Mountjoy Prison in 1942, he was released in the general amnesty of 1946; but the sentence does seem disproportionate to the crime.

The third notable incident in which Brendan Behan was vaguely associated with the I.R.A. follows the pattern of his Liverpool and Glasnevin involvements. Again, Behan seemed not to have been motivated by patriotism, but by what must finally be considered a rather stupid egotism. Any man who had spent six years in English prisons and who was under an English deportation order would be incredibly foolish to return to England at all. A man in this situation who would return to England with the most crudely faked identification to help an Irish prisoner escape from an English jail could have only been some sort of lunatic. Yet Brendan Behan, apparently not certifiably insane, traveled to England in 1947 to help Dick Timmons escape from prison; and Behan's account of his decision to go is almost tragic in its foolishness. According to Behan, he met a friend, a house painter named Michael O'Flaherty, in Grafton Street one day in 1947. O'Flaherty told Brendan that Dick Timmons wanted some help in getting out of jail. Behan remarked that he thought a good many people who were in jail would like to get out and laughed at O'Flaherty:

> Michael thought I was taking him for a right eejit and it didn't altogether please him.
> "This man happens to be a fellow citizen of yours, a Dublin man, born in Capel Street."
> Now I was reared a strict Dubliner and my mother was born in Capel Street so I felt a bit ashamed for having laughed.
> "Okay," I said, "surely I'll help." [41]

But Behan was as cautious and well prepared this time as he had been foolhardy and reckless before. From a friend named Barry O'Sullivan Behan obtained a passport; from yet another friend he obtained an R.A.F. identity card and paybook; and he also decided to carry a gun. He overlooked some small details, but even a most scrupulously careful man often fails to notice small matters which can spell the success or failure of a delicately complicated plan. O'Sullivan's passport stated that he had a glass eye. Who but the most boringly careful of planners would have noted that Behan had two good eyes and that his appearance generally did not coincide with the description on O'Sullivan's passport? Who but this same boringly careful planner would have advised Behan that he would be extremely lucky to sneak a revolver through customs? But any objective observer could easily see that the aforementioned difficulties were only small blemishes on an otherwise painstakingly planned endeavor.

With his revolver and his fake papers, Brendan Behan set forth from Dublin to Belfast. How carefully he traveled is attested to by the fact that the journey took him five days. Behan, in fact, traveled so cautiously that he arrived for embarkation a full day later than his papers allowed. Behan told the customs official he was delayed by his wife's pregnancy, and he was allowed to embark. Once on board the ship to England, probably in a clever attempt to disguise his being involved in a desperate prison break, Behan got very drunk. "I have discovered," he said, in describing this particular "bash," "no better way of doing your work as a soldier of the Irish Republic than by getting drunk." [42]

It is impossible to determine just exactly what Behan did, except get arrested, once he was in England. Behan himself gave little information on Dick Timmons' "escape": "Even at this stage of the game, it would not do to go into details as to how this was done. It was a highly organized operation and one that required a deal of planning and I would not like to spoil the game for others by shooting my mouth off now." [43] If, indeed, the operation was "highly organized," it would certainly have been a unique experience for Brendan Behan; and his reasons for not expanding on his part in helping Dick Timmons seem very strange. It was, after all, fifteen years after the incident that he recorded his reminiscences of it in *Confessions of an Irish Rebel.*

His reluctance, however, can be explained by Eoin O'Mahoney's account of Behan's part in Timmons' escape. O'Mahoney was in a position to know intimately the details of the case; for, when Behan was arrested in Manchester, it was O'Mahoney who flew from Ireland to defend him. According to O'Mahoney the prisoner had already escaped, or more properly, walked away from Leyhill open prison, before Behan arrived in England. The situation, then, was not so desperate as Behan would have had his audience believe, and again one is able to see the vast difference between what actually happened and what Behan, for purposes of publicity, wished the public to believe. Behan went to England and was arrested in Manchester simply because he was a reckless, foolish adventurer. His connection with the I.R.A. on this mission was highly informal. O'Mahoney puts it well: "Any organization which would employ Brendan to effect an escape should be examined by a mental expert." [44]

Brendan Behan was a rebel, but he was one mainly in the sense that the normal routine of an Irish house painter could not satisfy his immense vitality and reckless sense of adventure. The I.R.A., in the final analysis, seems to have been for Behan an excuse for doing what he probably would have done anyway. Surely, he generally sympathized with the aims of the I.R.A., but he was simply not the steely eyed gunman which the public, with Behan's complicity, insisted on believing he was. Sean Kavanaugh, Governor of Mountjoy while Behan was imprisoned there, mentions how he and others on the prison staff waited Brendan's arrival at the prison with a great deal of interest because of the sensational incident which had caused his arrest. Yet Kavanaugh reports that the Brendan Behan whom he and his staff expected was not by any means the same Behan who arrived: "Meeting this mild-mannered boy gave one a feeling of anti-climax; surely this was no desperado, no trigger-happy gunman. Even the fact that a sentence of fourteen years penal servitude was imposed on him a couple of weeks later by the Special Criminal Court for attempted murder did not lessen this feeling. The better one grew to know him the more the impression grew that basically he was a very gentle person who in his senses would not hurt a fly." [45]

Perhaps the saddest and most characteristic postscript to Behan's I.R.A. career is reported by Dominic Behan: "I remembered Brendan when he was drunk shortly before he died and he'd tell you the same story over and over, re-enacting the shooting for which he was sentenced to fourteen years in '42. 'I shot them! I shot them! I shot the bastards!' He had fired five rounds from a thirty-eight and missed with all five." [46] At this point, of course, Behan was completely the slave of the false image he had created for himself, but he was still misguidedly trying to reach back to the past in a desperate attempt to confirm that which he knew full well was false.

The difference between Behan's fiction and what actually happened indicates the vast disparity between the public image and the frightened man. Aware that he was telling lies about his life, Behan must have been afraid that he was also telling lies in his work; he must have been terribly afraid that his work, like his public image, was grounded upon the falsely sensational. A stronger man would have been able to use the public role for what it was worth and then discard it. Behan could not. In the last five years of his life the role played him.

VI *Behan and Prison*

Reckless, patently stupid and insane as Behan's I.R.A. missions were, he suffered severely for them. Brendan Behan spent most of his adolescence and early manhood in prison. The fact that he never quite grew up can certainly be blamed on these years in prison fully as much as upon that innate weakness which also existed in his character. Dominic puts it very well:

He didn't play for long under the street-lamp with us, for at the age of six he had joined the ranks of the young I.R.A. and by the very hour of his sixteenth birthday he was already in Walton Jail starting his first stretch. He was twenty-three years of age before they let him loose on the world, a man-boy with his first toy—freedom. Seeing life for the first time he grabbed everything with both hands and set about the job of living as an historian tackles the business of compressing centuries.[47]

The loneliness and forced restriction which Behan endured during his two long prison terms obviously haunted him. His inability to stop his mercurial rounds of Dublin and the world surely was a reaction to those many years during which his movement was severely restricted. Behan's greatest failure as a creative artist was, of course, his inability to isolate himself, wrestle with his talent, and get it down on paper. Too long restricted by prison, he could not endure the isolation which any creative artist must experience.

The most important aspect of Behan's years in prison, however, was the enlargement of his sympathies. His best friend in the Borstal institution was the English sailor, Charlie. In prison Behan learned that oppression cuts across geographic and social lines—that not only Irishmen went to prison—that men and boys could go to prison for crimes other than those directed against the English presence in Ireland. And to the credit of this man who could only imperfectly control the impulses of his own personality, he used his experiences in prison as the basis of two of his best works—Borstal Boy and The Quare Fellow. For one of the few times in his life Brendan Behan was able to turn the misfortunes he suffered into something of solid and lasting value, something beyond the beery anecdotes and songs belched out in barrooms in Dublin, Paris, and New York.

Behan's outlook was broadened in yet another way in prison, though it is doubtful that this experience, as insecure as he always was, helped his talent very much. Behan, who had been reared in the Catholic faith, was excommunicated in Walton Prison where he served part of his first sentence. After a confrontation with the prison priest, who, according to Behan, attacked him viciously for being a member of the I.R.A. and forbade him communion, he was hustled back to his cell. He reports that the guards beat him severely; and, even though Behan may have added a few dramatic touches to his encounter with the priest and the guards, his description of his despair at his excommunication is obviously authentic:

I sat down on the chair and leaned my head in my hands. I felt like crying for the first time in years, for the first time since I was a kid of four or five. I had often prayed after Mass at home that God would not let me lose the Faith. I thought of Sister Monica, the old nun that prepared me for my first Confession and Communion and Confirmation, and Father Campbell, the old priest in Gardiner Street that I went to Confession to, and Christmas numbers of the little holy books we used to have at home. Never, never no more.[48]

VII   *The Catacombs and MacDaid's*

Another important influence on Behan the man and Behan the writer was the group of friends which he made shortly upon his release from prison in 1946. Alan Simpson, who produced *The Quare Fellow,* was a member of this group; and he describes its activities well: "In the Paris of the nineteenth century they used to be called 'Bohemians.' In the Dublin of the late forties and early fifties, it was the 'MacDaids's crowd'." [49] The tag, "the MacDaid's crowd" came from the pub in which the group gathered—John MacDaid's establishment at 3 Harry Street, Dublin. MacDaid's pub, according to an advertisement in *Envoy* magazine, was a place where "the drink is efficacious and the conversation effervescent." [50] The efficacious drink and effervescent conversation quite often overflowed the bounds of MacDaid's pub, and after closing hours, the party which had started in the tavern was moved to "The Catacombs," the basement of a large Georgian house an easy walk from MacDaid's.

The proprietor of "The Catacombs" was a former London nightclub manager who had transferred his managerial talents to Dublin. Not solely out of interest for the intellectual and alcholic welfare of his guests, however, did the major-domo of "The Catacombs" throw open his doors to the MacDaid's group. He was genuinely interested in paying his rent and in having a bit left over, and to effect this end he rented sections of "The Catacombs" to those who desired privacy. In addition, he claimed as his due the deposit money on all the empty bottles after the revelers departed.

Dominic Behan gives a hilarious account of a party in "The Catacombs" which ended in a net loss for the manager. The discussion of the assembled party had ascended to the level of observing that someone had ruined Bertie's print of the "Naked Maja" by adding a fig leaf. Words failed the outraged discussants, and they took action by throwing their empties at the defaced print:

"Unforgivable," said Podmore, and flung a Guinness bottle at the print and the glass splintered on the stone floor. Newman thought it a great game and threw a bottle. So did Kathy and Liz and everybody else, and in a little while the ground below the print was littered with broken glass over which Bertie was weeping drunkenly. "My rent," he wept, "my rent, and I did mind you so well."

"What's he on about?" I asked Brendan, who was making for the door leading to the street. "The bottles," he replied, "Bertie would have made a couple of quid on the refund. That's why he holds parties at all. And you, yeh eejit, yeh couldn't even prevent that. C'mon, and we'll get home outa this. Have yeh the price of a taxi?" I said I had. "C'mon then, before yeh break somethin' else." [51]

MacDaid's advertisement was true, assuming he did not water down the alcoholic offerings; for the people who gathered at the pub from time to time insured effervescent conversation. The group included the writers Anthony Cronin and J. P. Donleavy, both of whom drew upon the experiences of the MacDaid's group in their writing: Cronin in *The Life of Riley* and Donleavy in the more widely known *Ginger Man*. Other well-known members of the MacDaid's group were John Ryan, artist, generous patron of the arts, and co-founder of the important though short-lived Irish literary magazine *Envoy;* Alan Simpson, founder of Dublin's Pike Theatre and producer of Behan's *The Quare Fellow;* and, of course, Behan himself, who probably was happier and more at ease during his association with the MacDaid's group than at any other time in his life. He had no name as yet, so his friends had no reason to be jealous of him. He did not have sufficient money to stay drunk for more than a healthy two to three hours a day. He was surrounded by a group of people fully as intelligent and tough-minded as himself, and he could not badger them into according him a position of false self-importance.

How important was Behan's association with the group he met in MacDaid's and in "The Catacombs" is attested to by the fact that one of Behan's earliest serious publications, a short story entitled "A Woman of No Standing," appeared in John Ryan's *Envoy.* More important, of course, is Behan's association with Alan Simpson. Had Simpson not been able to see the vitality and truth of Behan's play, which had already been rejected by Radio Éireann and the Abbey Theatre, Behan could have been a good deal longer in coming to the attention of the public. The contacts which Behan made during this period of life were indeed valuable, then, and not only, as Alan Simpson puts it, "in the material sense, but the effect of the example of others trying to express something new, through writing, painting, or music." [52]

VIII   *Early Writing Efforts*

It would be a mistake to assume that, without his association with the MacDaid's group, Brendan Behan's writing talent would have remained latent. Simpson says that at the time he first knew Behan, he had "no thoughts of being a playwright. . . . Brendan was interested, as most of us were at that time, purely in drinking, politics and parties." [53] Simpson's conclusion is certainly a logical one, and one which Behan's pub behavior reinforced. Yet, Simpson's conclusions about Behan's writing ambitions are incorrect. At least four years before he fell in with the MacDaid's group, Behan had tried his hand at playwriting. The play which resulted from this effort was entitled *The Landlady;* and, though it was by all accounts not a very good play, it is one important case in point in the argument that Behan took a serious view of his writing, and had done so long before he rocketed to world fame. Jimmy Bourke, Behan's cousin, gives the following account of *The Landlady:*

"The Landlady" by Brendan Behan was I believe the first play he ever wrote. It was written when he was in Mountjoy in 1943? He went there after Easter 1942, and was there at least eighteen months. I agreed to have the manuscript typed. It was a rather long play in three acts of a hundred typed pages, double spacing. There was the original and copy, and Brendan's holograph and these in a parcel were returned to the author by post. I soon regretted doing this, because Brendan was most untidy and I believe no copy of the play exists. One copy was sent by him to the Group Theatre in Belfast. It may not have arrived and might have been seized by the authorities. I asked Governor Sean Kavanagh and he does not remember the play at all. He said anyway when a prisoner left all his belongings would have been given to him. Brendan left Mountjoy for Arbour Hill, the Military Detention Prison, with his comrades. I am informed by a companion of Brendan's that Mountjoy was more conducive to writing and reading and study generally than Arbour Hill.

The play had little action. It concerned The Landlady, his grandmother Christine English (she had been married twice), whom I remember as a splendid figure of a matron, a matriarch with luxuriant black hair. When she lay dead at sixty six (?) her hair was in two big black braids by her side. The play was a slice of life seen through the eyes of a little boy . . . a precocious boy, Brendan himself, who was in the play more or less as a listener. Granny was sick in bed in the first act and the neighbors, tenants, friends, inebriates, holy and unholy people trouped in to beg or borrow and to pay their rent. A bucket of porter stood handy and almost everyone who came in imbibed. There was a girl living in Russell Street, the setting of the play, who was pregnant and her lover was unwilling to marry her. She tried to commit suicide by cutting her throat with a razor. Auntie Kathleen Behan (Brendan's mother) FLEW FOR THE POLICE when she discovered the girl in the lavatory in her gore. This made a headline in the papers of the day and it was an incident in Brendan's play. He had the girl actually cutting her throat ON STAGE. In my criticism of the play at the time I pointed out to Brendan that this should be done OFF STAGE, that it would be difficult and melodramatic to show ON STAGE. In my criticism generally I said Brendan was seeing his play through the eyes of himself as a small child. His ear was unerring, the dialogue was good, but there was not sufficient action. I regarded it as [an] exercise. Indeed I suggested to Brendan that he should devote his talents to writing stories, novels, and not write for the stage. In saying this I clearly said, after my own discouraging experience with the knuckle heads running the theatre in Dublin, Brendan was wasting his time.[54]

Behan himself, in 1954, when he was still lucid and able to judge his own work, referred to The Landlady by saying "Anything written in jail is plain rubbish, and that includes Pilgrim's Progress." [55] Whether the play was much good or not, however, is irrelevant. That Behan wrote the play at all is indisputable evidence that many years before The Quare Fellow and Borstal Boy Behan was transferring to paper his impressions of the Dublin he knew so well. More important, neither money nor publicity was involved in the writing of *The Landlady*.

But *The Landlady* was by no means Behan's first attempt at writing. Just as he was born an Irishman, a Republican, and a Catholic, he seems also to have been born a writer. As early as June, 1936, "Breandain O Beachain" had published a story called "A Tantalising Tale" in the short-lived Irish periodical *Fianna*. The story is not much better than what one would expect from an intelligent thirteen-year-old, but it is interesting in that it demonstrates that the child is father of the man. Not only does "A Tantalising Tale" indicate Behan's early interest in writing, it indicates something of the mature Behan's ambitions and the nature of the subject matter with which he was later to deal. "A Tantalising Tale" is told by the narrator to four much younger companions:

"You ought to have some story worth relating," said the young Kerry O/C as we sat in my library after the Fianna Ard Fheis. I was not long returned from America and had purchased—and settled down in—a large and comfortable house. As I had, if anything, more room than I needed, I was proud to offer accommodations and hospitality to four of the country delegates.

I was out, you see, in the '67 Rising and had to clear the country, like many a better man. But the long years in the States had not changed my outlook and views, and I had been heart and soul with the men of '16 and '22. I had always had a great admiration for the young lads of Na Fianna Éireann. With Mellowes, I believed that their "ideal would save the future." Anyway, I supported them morally and financially—a surprising thing, you will, maybe, say in one who is almost a millionaire! Yes, you have guessed it. I am the J. Frank O'Brien, known "across the pond" as the oil king.[56]

The mature Behan, of course, had a house in a well-to-do Dublin suburb; and he, too, offered accommodation and hospitality to all who would listen to his tantalizing tales. In any case, the story which the narrator tells deals with a mysterious ring which is given to him by a dying Parisian. The narrator, the same evening he receives the ring, is bundled out of a restaurant when the waiter serving him notices the ring with "an expression of horror." Because the narrator protests on being thrown out of the restaurant, he is arrested and taken to a police station. He is questioned, and the police decide to hold him overnight; but, "Realising that

any delay would upset my plans and those of my comrades, I
determined to escape, if I could. So, as I was being led to the cells,
I drew a pistol on my custodians and was gone before they recov-
ered from their surprise. Luckily, we left for Bordeaux next morning and in a few weeks time were safe in New York." [57] In New
York, the narrator is questioned about the ring by a professor
whose acquaintance he makes. When the narrator searches the
box in which he has locked the strange ring, the ring is gone:

"No, my lads, I never found it but I do pity the poor fellow who
did . . ."
The delegates started as my yarn abruptly finished. Then they
looked at each other and grinned. It was certainly, they agreed, a tantalising tale.[58]

After building up the mysterious nature of the ring, thirteen-
year-old Brendan Behan was unable to find a suitable conclusion.
Some of Behan's severer critics would claim that Behan never out-
grew this inability to create an esthetically acceptable conclusion,
for of the three major works which Behan wrote—*Borstal Boy*,
The Quare Fellow, The Hostage—only *The Quare Fellow* possesses a conclusion which is easily justifiable. But whether Behan
indeed did ever learn to write conclusions or not, "A Tantalising
Tale" gives credence to Behan's statement: "If I am anything at
all, I am a man of letters. I'm a writer: a word which does not
exactly mean anything in either the English, Irish or American
language. But I have never seen myself as anything else, not even
from the age of six when my mother says that when she sent me
for a loaf of bread, I used to kick a piece of paper along the street
in front of me so that I could read it." [59]
In the Borstal institution, Behan, by his own account, also
evinced his desire to write. When there was to be an Eisteddfod, a
variation on the traditional Welsh competition in music and poetry, Behan passed up all the other competition—in athletics,
handicraft, and gardening—in favor of "an essay competition on
the subject 'My Home Town.' One hundred Players [cigarettes]
was the prize and that, I said in my own mind, is my hundred
Players." [60] Perhaps the competition was not terribly severe, yet
Behan won; and he worked diligently on his essay, though he admitted the subject was an easy one: "I worked very hard at my
essay nearly every evening in my exercise book; writing a first

draft and a second before I'd put it down on the foolscap." [61] Unfortunately, when Behan was older, he sometimes did not work with as much discipline as he did as a youth in prison.

IX *Behan the Writer*

Behan had learned the value of hard work in prison. Sean Kavanaugh is of the opinion that Behan's years in prison, especially the last four years, were the time when he did most of his writing,[62] but Kavanaugh is probably not correct, for the evidence suggests that Behan did a good deal of writing after his release. Yet Behan could only write well when he was able to impose upon himself that control which he had learned in prison. During the last five years, Behan could not discipline himself in even the most elementary sense; and it is unfortunate that this picture of the messy, offensive drunkard is the one that is likely to survive. Yet, if this is the picture of Behan which does survive, it will not do justice to the man; for he did have talent, and at one time he knew how to discipline it. He rewrote *Borstal Boy* several times, and the first three-quarters of the book is evidence enough that Behan knew the discipline necessary for good writing.

Rae Jeffs, speaking of that section of the *Borstal Boy* manuscript which she saw the first time she met Behan says, "if the man himself was undisciplined, certainly his work was not. It was clean and well typed, and what corections there were—and there were few—were written neatly and precisely in his own hand. It is more than a pity that by his own wish all but a few pages of this manuscript have been destroyed, for it would have supplied one further piece of evidence of his contradictory nature." [63]

Another evidence of Behan's ability to do hard work and his general respect for his writing is seen in the history of *The Quare Fellow*. The play was written first as a one-act radio play in Gaelic and was called *Casadh Súgáin Eile—The Twisting of Another Rope*. When Behan could not place this version with Radio Éireann, he rewrote the play for the stage and submitted it to the MacLiammoir-Edwards company at the Gate Theatre, and then to the Abbey Theatre. Both companies rejected the play; and, on receiving the Abbey's rejection, Behan compared himself to Joyce and O'Casey: "God dammit, you might as well be out of this world as out of the fashion, for didn't Joyce and O'Casey have their plays rejected one time?" [64]

Behan rewrote the play and submitted it once more to the Abbey. It was again rejected, though the Abbey producer did admit that in the last form in which the play was submitted it would be stageable if Behan would revise the characters of the Mountjoy Prison warders sufficiently to avoid the libel charges that could be brought against the Abbey. Behan, though irritated, bided his time until Alan Simpson decided to produce the play. After Simpson accepted the play, changes were made, including the important one of substituting the title *The Quare Fellow* for *The Twisting of Another Rope*. Behan talked little of these changes, yet the fact remains that he reworked his script at least three times before he arrived at the final version which Simpson produced. To describe some of Behan's later work (*Brendan Behan's New York*, for instance) as hit or miss would be giving it a compliment; to describe his earlier work in this way is distinctly unjustified.

Approximately a year before *The Quare Fellow* was produced, Behan had published serially in the *Irish Times* a short novel entitled *The Scarperer;* and, though the novel is by no means one of the most substantial in the language, it is yet another indication of Behan's ability to pursue an honest job of work. In 1953 Behan was still aware that, in order to get his writing done, he had to isolate himself from the temptations of the Dublin pubs. To complete *The Scarperer* he went to the Aran Islands and with only a few interruptions worked steadily until the novel was finished. The *Times Literary Supplement*, in its recent review of *The Scarperer*, recognizes the workmanlike quality of the novel, calling Behan "a conscientious craftsman who did a good job for his market," a writer who did a "professional job." [65] The reviewer damns Behan with faint praise, but the important element in the review is the emphasis on Behan as a "professional" and a "craftsman."

In the early days, Behan worked hard at his writing, and everything concerned with it interested him. With his last few books, however, he cared not at all about his work. At the last the only thing that could pierce through Behan's sickness was the fact that any book bearing Brendan Behan's name could make money. Before drink and his psychological problems drove him to madness, he worried and fussed about the title of one of his books. In 1957, only after an extended review of several alternative titles did

Behan finally settle on *Borstal Boy* for his autobiographical work. In 1962 he not only cared little about what appeared on the cover of his books, he cared little about what was between the covers. *Brendan Behan's Island* is an excellent example. After the tapes were edited, the assembled text was not long enough to fill out the required number of pages. Rae Jeffs called Behan in New York to advise him that, to complete the text, some of the material he had already published would have to be included. When Mrs. Jeffs listed the material she thought was suitable, Behan offered no advice, no opinion. He had completely lost all creative desire and capability. As Rae Jeffs says, Brendan Behan at this point might as well have been dead; for as a writer he was.

The Behan of those last years was not the real Behan, not the man who was sincerely interested in his work for its own sake and who was serious enough about his writing to make considerable sacrifice for it. On September 20, 1957, shortly after the completed manuscript of *Borstal Boy* was finally in the hands of the publishers, Behan wrote to Iain Hamilton. In the letter, quoted in full in Rae Jeffs's book, Behan asserts an overwhelming confidence in his ability to produce serious work: "I miss my poor old book [*Borstal Boy*] though long and lovingly I cussed it. However, there's more where that came from as the mother of twenty said." [66] Behan then describes a newspaper job which he has turned down in order to continue with his playwriting. He also mentions a novel called *the catacombs* (lower case intentional) which he intends to start "in a couple of weeks." The newspaper job was apparently a good one which would have consisted of some routine reporting and would have assured Behan a regular Sunday column in the Irish edition of the *People*. Perhaps it was unwise for him to refuse this job, for the discipline of daily reporting might have given his life some of the order which it so desperately needed. Such speculation aside, Behan was willing at this time to sacrifice for his art.

X *The Last Sad Days*

The intervals of clarity and sobriety became fewer as the pressures which drove Behan were more and more able to work their will unimpeded upon him. The publishers who collected neither the money nor the books Behan died owing them must have had a difficult time sorting the genius from the fraud. There were possibly obligations which will never come to light, but the ones which Mrs. Jeffs lists are overwhelming enough to indicate the hopeless morass into which Behan had worked himself. He had obligated himself to several books he had no capability of finishing unaided. *Brendan Behan's New York* and *Confessions of an Irish Rebel* Rae Jeffs managed to pull together from tapes which Behan had made for her. The *Irish Press* articles were published as *Hold Your Hour and Have Another*. Mrs. Jeffs could not, however, help Behan to finish the rest of the crazy quilt which he had constructed.

In addition to the books already mentioned, he had signed a contract with G. P. Putnam to produce a book on himself, a book of photographs each of which was to be captioned by Behan. He had also contracted with Doubleday for a book on the Irish Revolution. For each book, he had received a $3000 advance, which, needless to say, he promptly spent. Behan died, then, owing a great deal; but, though the publishers suffered, the world could never repay what Behan had given.

Brendan Behan reminded the human being of his vitality, reminded him that there is a lot to be enjoyed in the interval between the cradle and the grave, that even though most causes come to nought, man can achieve a certain qualified dignity through belief. He believed; he fought (most inefficiently); he would not remain silent; death finally caught up with him, but Behan put up a magnificent struggle. As Brian Behan has stated,

Standing opposite Brendan are the thousands of lemmings who march on to their deaths without ever doing a single thing to alter their unhappy states. His end is preferable to their mummification. I'm damn sure a world where the Brendans would rule would be a lot better than the crazy, stupid chaotic one that we live in now. In the end there was nothing left for him to do but die, and like everything else he did, he carried it to excess. . . . He was too big for his own skin. A lesser man might have peeped out at the world and made notes. Brendan jumped into it and gave that old triangle a mighty swipe.[67]

CHAPTER 2

Some Relevant Theories of Comedy

> And if I laugh at any mortal thing
> 'Tis that I may not weep
> —Lord Byron, *Don Juan*

BRENDAN Behan claimed "a sense of humor that would cause me to laugh at a funeral, providing it wasn't my own." [1] This peculiar juxtaposition of laughter and death is an element found in most of Behan's work—in fact, it could be said to be his most characteristic theme. Some reviewers have called it "gallows humor," "tasteless and macabre"; Sam Hynes calls it "the tough con's protective refusal to expose himself through emotion." [2] If this assessment is correct, then this "tough con" has not covered his feelings well enough; for in Behan's two major plays the feelings of the characters and of their creator regularly break through the comic surface. Those who might see Behan as merely a drunken funny man are evidently not sensitive enough to realize that a good deal of the comedy in Behan's plays portrays the hysteria which overcomes the human being caught in a situation over which he has no control. And it seems that most of those critics who condemn Behan for his less-than-somber approach do not understand very well either the general functions of comedy or Behan's particular application of them.[3]

I *Representative Theories of Comedy*

It is presumptuous, of course, for anyone to claim that he understands fully all the subtleties of comic theory and technique. As Paul Lauter says in his anthology of comic theory, "Critics have never tired of complaining that comic theory is no laughing matter; unfortunately, the stock-in-trade of those who have written about comic theorists has been little more than a weary joke. And while there have been a few honorable exceptions to the

55

habit of simply lampooning the theorists, fewer still have been the
serious attempts to arrange speculations about comedy in some
coherent pattern." [4] Groucho Marx has been quoted as saying:
"There are all kinds of humor. Some is derisive, some sympathetic,
and some merely whimsical. That is what makes comedy so much
harder to create than serious drama; people laugh in many different ways, and they cry in only one." [5] And one must agree with
William McCollom that "A good joke is as rich in overtones as a
good metaphor and puts up as much resistance to simple interpretation." [6] Certainly tragedy is not inherently easier to analyze
than comedy, but at least one has Aristotle's cogent pronouncements to use as touchstone on the former.

Concerning comedy, however, only a few of Aristotle's state-
ments have survived. He did say that comedy "aims at presenting
men as worse, tragedy as better than in actual life" and that comedy is "an imitation of characters of a lower type; it does not,
however, involve the full range of villainy, but only the ludicrous,
a subdivision of the ugly or base. The ludicrous consists in some
defect or ugliness which is not painful or destructive. To take an
obvious example, the comic mask is ugly and distorted but does
not give pain." [7] Brief, however, as Aristotle's pronouncements on
comedy are his emphasis upon the ugly and the deformed as
comic represents a useful early classification, and one that has
been much imitated. Cicero, for example, says that the comic "lies
in a certain baseness and deformity; for those sayings are laughed
at solely or chiefly which point out and designate something
offensive in an inoffensive manner." [8] Aristotle implies the instructive nature of the comic. Other early theorists of comedy comment
explicitly on its corrective powers. Donatus saw comedy as "a
fable involving diverse arrangements of civic and private concerns, in which one learns what is useful in life and what on the
contrary is to be avoided." [9] A critic of the Italian Renaissance,
Lucio Olimpio Giraldi, writing on Terence, also emphasizes comedy as instruction: "Terence's intention was to show the ugliness
of foul things so that men would abstain from them, not so that
they would follow them; and to propose to them the praiseworthy
and virtuous and honest ones so that they might embrace them
and adorn themselves with them. Just as tragedy purges men's
minds, through terror and pity, and induces men to abstain from

acting wickedly, so comedy, by means of laughter and jokes, calls men to an honest private life." [10]

Some of the earliest English theorists also called attention, with the Puritan attacks on the theater as a catalyst, to the instructive nature of comedy. Ben Jonson, in his "Dedicatory Epistle to Volpone" says that it is "the office of a comic poet to imitate justice and instruct to life" [11] and that dramatists who practice "ribaldry, profanation, blasphemy, all license of offence to God and man" employ these devices the better to instruct the audience in virtue. Certainly, though Behan has been accused of the same offenses against God and man that Jonson and his contemporaries were accused of committing, it would be rather farfetched to assume that Behan wrote his plays solely to instruct his audience. It would, however, be equally inaccurate to assume that Behan did not intend in *The Quare Fellow, The Hostage, Borstal Boy,* and in various of his minor works to ridicule the pretensions of mankind, and thus by implication instruct the audience as to what it ought not to be. Behan would agree with Bergson, who saw laughter as being "intended to humiliate, it must make a painful impression on the person against whom it is directed." [12]

II *Laughter as Satire*

Behan had a fine eye for the ridiculous in human behavior, as evidenced by his creation of such characters as the shallowly pious Holy Healy in *The Quare Fellow* and the absurdly chauvinistic Monsewer in *The Hostage.* It is equally evident that Behan exhibits neither these characters nor others of their sort for emulation. Behan had an accurate and unfailing sympathy for the human being as he was, and as he ought to be; and in his writings, those who dehumanize themselves, those who become slave to their pretensions and would, thus, harm other human beings, bring down upon themselves all the comic scorn Behan can muster. James K. Feibelman describes this aspect of comedy in his *Aesthetics:* "Always . . . the situation must illustrate the absence of what ought to be, if it is to reveal comedy. The unexpected indication of the absence of perfection (the *ought*) constitutes the comic situation." [13] Behan is aware of the "absence of perfection" in his world, but his sympathy for the people who inhabit it is undimmed; George Meredith, in *An Essay on Comedy,* describes this ability as follows: "You may estimate your capability for Comic perception by being able to detect the ridicule of them you love without loving them less." [14] And truly, though Behan ridiculed the Irish in particular and the human being in general, he was always in love with life and humanity.

George Santayana also expresses some ideas about the comic which seem most relevant to Behan's special genius:

Reason, taken psychologically, is an old inherited passion like any other, the passion for consistency and order; and it is just as prone as the other passions to overstep the modesty of nature and to regard its own aims as alone important. But this is ridiculous; because importance springs from the stress of nature, from the cry of life, not from reason and its pale prescriptions. Reason cannot stand alone; brute habit and blind play are at the bottom of art and morals, and unless irrational impulses and fancies are kept alive, the life of reason collapses for sheer emptiness.[15]

Santayana's remarks might serve well to describe the absurd sort of inhuman quasi-logic which is one of the prime concerns of *The Quare Fellow*. Obviously only an overindulged passion for order at any cost can be used to justify the taking of one life for another, or the differentiation between a murderer who has killed his wife with a silver-topped cane and one who has killed his brother and afterwards sliced up the body. In *The Quare Fellow*, the man who killed his wife is pardoned and the man who killed his brother is hanged—logical, if one proceeds from rather absurd first principles; the absurdity of those first principles, and the stupidity of the resulting "logic" is emphasized and laughed at by Behan.

III   *Comedy as Celebration*

Brendan Behan was a man well acquainted with the tragic aspects of human existence, having spent many years of his life in prison, and having been born into a country where a man's self-respect was also synonymous with the foolhardy notion that the only honorable death could come in a struggle against the British. How could this man, so involved with so much unhappiness, write comedy? Again, Santayana is helpful, for his "Carnival," written over thirty years before Behan became well known, might well describe the dominant theme in both *The Quare Fellow* and *The*

Hostage: "In the jumble of existence there must be many a knock and many a grief; people living at cross purposes cannot be free from malice, and they must needs be fooled by their pretentious passions. But there is no need of taking these evils tragically. At bottom they are gratuitous, and might have been avoided if people had not pledged their hearts to things beyond their control and had not entrenched themselves in their illusions." [10] Laughter, says Santayana, is the proper answer for those who ask that their pretentious illusions concerning the somberness of life be taken seriously. Behan would agree.

Susanne Langer's theory of comedy, which recognizes the assertion of human vitality characteristic of comedy, also seems relevant to Behan's writings:

Comedy is an art form that arises naturally wherever people are gathered to celebrate life, in spring festivals, triumphs, birthdays, weddings, or initiations, for it expresses the elementary strains and resolutions of animate nature, the animal drives that persist even in human nature, the delight man takes in his special gifts that make him the lord of creation; it is an image of human vitality holding its own in the world amid the surprises of unplanned coincidence. The most obvious occasions for the performance of comedies are thanks or challenges to fortune. What justifies the term "Comedy" is not that the ancient ritual procession, the Comus, honoring the god of that name, was the source of this great art form—for comedy has arisen in many parts of the world, where the Greek god with his particular worship was unknown —but that the Comus was a fertility rite, and the god it celebrated a fertility god, a symbol of perpetual rebirth, eternal life.[17]

Or, as Behan puts it at the end of *The Hostage*, when the young hostage who has been killed jumps up and sings:

> The bells of hell
> Go ting-a-ling-a-ling
> For you but not for me.
> Oh death where is thy
> Sting-a-ling-a-ling
> Or grave thy victory?
> If you meet the undertaker
> Or the young man from the Pru,
> Get a pint with what's left over
> Now I'll say goodbye to you.[18]

What Miss Langer says about "gallows humor" is also relevant
to the special sort of comedy found in Behan's plays: "In so-called
'gallows humor'—the harsh laugh in distress—the 'lift' of vital
feeling is simply a flash of self-assertion. Something similar probably causes the mirthless laughter of hysterics: in the disorganized
response of a hysterical person, the sense of vitality breaks
through fear and depression spasmodically, so that it causes ex-
plosive laughter, sometimes alternating with sobs and tears." [19]

Eric Bentley, in *The Life of the Drama,* makes a related point:

We conventionally consider comedy a gay and lighthearted form of art,
and we regard any contrasting element as secondary, an undertone,
an interruption, an exception. I am proposing, instead, to regard misery
as the basis of comedy and gaiety as an ever-recurring transcendence.
Seen in this way, comedy, like tragedy, is a way of trying to cope with
despair, mental suffering, guilt and anxiety. But not in the same way.
. . . The comic poet does not speak his feelings directly but veils
them, contradicts them with pranks or elegancies. . . . Comedy is
indirect, ironical. It says fun when it means misery. And when it lets
the misery show, it is able to transcend it in joy.[20]

IV Behan's Comic Genius

In general, Behan's comedy exhibits both the satiric and the
assertive impulses. Behan satirizes man's stupidity; at the same
time, he says that the human being will endure, is too vital to be
destroyed even by his only foolishness.

Behan's satire presumes, as does all satire, a disparity between
the real—man as he is, and the ideal—man as he ought to be.
Behan's countryman Swift, reflecting the ideals of his age, writes
about men who are ridiculous because they fail to be reasonable.
Behan, countering the death wish of his age, writes about men
who are ridiculous because they fail intellectually and emotionally
to realize the basic worth of human life. "It's a queer world," says
Behan, "but the best we've got to be going on with"; and those
who become involved in their own petty schemes, whether these
rise from the intellect or the emotions, are mercilessly satirized by
Behan.

In this respect, Behan is very much aware of the societal and
theatrical developments of his time. Martin Esslin, in his excellent
The Theatre of the Absurd, says that absurdist drama "castigates,

satirically, the absurdity of lives lived unaware and unconscious of ultimate reality," lives which exclude humanity as they allow themselves to become prisoners of "inauthentic, petty society." [21] This is exactly the type of satire Behan writes.

Both Behan and playwrights better known as practitioners of the "theatre of the absurd" go beyond criticism of the hollowness of the society which man has created. With Samuel Beckett, Albert Camus, Eugene Ionesco, Jean Genet, and Jean-Paul Sartre, Behan realizes the basic absurdity of man's condition; he realizes that man is thrown into a world which he can neither control nor understand; and Behan's answer, like that of his contemporaries, is laughter. This laughter is at the same time a protest and a triumph. Perceiving the disparity between the world as it is and the world as he can imagine it, the man aware of the absurd laughs; and in this laugh he protests that he is superior to the world because he possesses the power to imagine it as something better than it is. The laugh also asserts man's vitality, his refusal to accept the sentence which the world passes on him, his assertion that he will stay in the game even though he is aware of the final score.

In his classic essay "The Myth of Sisyphus," after rejecting suicide as the answer to the senselessness of man's existence, Camus chooses to see something hopeful in the situation of Sisyphus, condemned by the gods to the never ending task of rolling a huge rock up a mountain only to have it roll down again. Camus can imagine Sisyphus happy, and can also imagine no fate which cannot be surmounted by scorn. This happiness—this scorn—is the substance of the laughter in Behan's writing.

Robert Corrigan, commenting on the state of modern theater in general and describing in particular the new and peculiar dramatic form sometimes called "absurdist," explains how comedy is derived from a situation which could, perhaps more reasonably, cause deep despair: "When man is forced to admit that the absurd is more than ever inherent in human existence, when he sees his existence as essentially governed by the irrational, the inexplicable, the nonsensical, he moves into the realm of the comic. For comedy supposes an unformed world, a world being made and turned upside down. In our Punch and Judy world no one is guilty or responsible. As Gautier put it, 'comedy is the logic of the absurd.' . . ." [22] It is absurd that the creature who has so little time wastes it by destroying his fellows, says Behan; and it is absurd that the creature who can imagine everything must certainly come to nothing. Brendan Behan's comedies, satiric and assertive, say two things: man is ridiculous; man is alive and will endure.

CHAPTER 3

The Quare Fellow

> I didn't write this play; the lags wrote it.
> —Brendan Behan, after the opening
> night of *The Quare Fellow*

IT is impossible to say exactly when Behan began *The Quare Fellow*, but it was probably sometime in 1952. Certainly he had completed the play well before December, 1954, when it opened at Dublin's tiny Pike Theatre under the direction of Alan Simpson. Before the play was accepted by Simpson, Behan had been making the rounds for some time trying to get it produced. As has been noted, the B.B.C., Radio Éireann, and the Abbey Theatre had rejected Behan's play. In one of its earlier forms, the play was very short, consisting only of the events surrounding the hangman's coming to the jail. In one of its later versions, *The Quare Fellow* was so long that it would have taken four hours to play.[1] It was essentially this impractically long version of *The Quare Fellow* which Alan Simpson accepted for production and which his wife Carolyn helped Behan to cut to the form in which the script now exists.

I Stage History

Had Behan had an opportunity to choose an ideal producer for his play, he could have done no better than Alan Simpson. Simpson had been stage manager for Hilton Edwards and Michael MacLiammor, and he had gained in this and other associations with theater a broad and varied experience. He knew just how to handle *The Quare Fellow*, and he turned the twelve-by-twelve-foot Pike Theatre stage into a positive advantage:

For the size of the theatre, I was able to have, comparatively speaking, much more lighting equipment than would be possible in a larger

63

building, and, by its use, minimized the difficulties caused by the close proximity of the audience to the stage and the smallness of the stage itself. I used a method of lighting which I had learnt from watching ballet: this was to light from directly overhead and from the side, only using sufficient front lighting to heighten slightly the amount of light on the actors' faces. All the lighting I used was directional: that is to say, there was no spilling or flooding of light over the stage and, by this method, I achieved a three-dimensional emphasis on the actors which made the stage look bigger than it really was. . . . I achieved something in the nature of a 3-D theatre, making the audience feel they were a part of the play and involving them in its action and atmosphere. . . . This is borne out by the back-handed tributes of several "old-lag" friends of Brendan's, who declared that they really felt they were "inside" again while watching *The Quare Fellow*.[2]

The stage of the Pike was unbelievably small; the auditorium had only fifty-five seats. But *The Quare Fellow*'s first night was by no means a shoddy, fly-by-night sort of affair. Simpson and his accomplished cast gave the play a highly professional, polished performance. Nor was the play ignored by the newspaper critics. The *Irish Press* and the *Irish Times* were both represented, the former by no less a critic than Lennox Robinson, who, though he did not praise the play highly, admitted that it had some good moments and that the acting was superb. Robinson's faint praise might have been qualified a bit, however, by the Abbey's having already rejected the play. A widely circulated anecdote has it that during the intermission Gabriel Fallon of the *Dublin Evening Press* asked Lennox Robinson whether he was enjoying the play. "My dear fellow," Robinson is said to have replied, "how can you possibly expect me to enjoy a play I turned down." [3] Whether this anecdote is true or not, it is so commonly repeated that it has become a part of the lore of the first night of *The Quare Fellow*. Other reviews, notably one by Gabriel Fallon, were much more enthusiastic, praising the play for its vitality and perceptiveness. Some felt that Fallon praised Behan's play too highly, but ten years after his enthusiastic review of *The Quare Fellow*, Fallon still had not recanted his opinion that *The Quare Fellow* demonstrated that Behan had in him the stuff of another O'Casey.[4]

The Quare Fellow ran for four weeks at the Pike and would probably have run much longer except for economic factors. Many of the actors had to return to the security of their regular jobs; and, though the fifty-five-seat theater was filled each night, Simpson reports that the production was not breaking even—it was losing, in fact, a half pound or so every week.[5] The best efforts of Simpson and Behan to locate the play after it had closed at the Pike were discouraging. Whether because of Behan's reputation or because of timid Irish Puritanism, no theater in Dublin would take *The Quare Fellow;* and the next production of the play was in London a year and a half later. On May 24, 1956, *The Quare Fellow* opened at the Theatre Royal, Stratford, East London, under the direction of Joan Littlewood; and this production brought Behan world fame. Unfortunately, the fame which he achieved was not solely a result of his play, for it was during the run of *The Quare Fellow* at Stratford that Behan appeared, sloppily and incoherently drunk, on Malcolm Muggeridge's television program "Panorama."

In spite of the fact that *The Quare Fellow* was not very widely noticed until Behan's television performance, the play was well received by the critics. Kenneth Tynan's review in the *London Observer* for May 25, 1956, is an example. The *London Times* noted the sprawling structure of the play but admitted, reluctantly, that the laughter, the satire, and the theme of social indignation were effectively presented. Joan Littlewood's consummate production skills, of course, had much to do with the London success of *The Quare Fellow,* but it is unfair to Behan to overestimate Miss Littlewood's role. She made the play a wonderful production, but so did Alan Simpson before her. Both producers, though they made many changes, were working with the script that Behan, not they, had written. Many of Behan's harsher critics, most of them pretentiously intellectual Irishmen, assert that Behan's writings were solely the product of many hard-working producers and indulgent friends. If such were the case, it is indeed strange that those who did Behan's work for him have not produced anything worthwhile since his death.

The Quare Fellow ran for six months under Joan Littlewood's sure hand; and, since the British had put their stamp of approval on the play, it was allowed back into Ireland where it was produced at the Abbey in October, 1956. Behan had had other offers for a second Dublin performance, but he had turned them down in favor of the Abbey. Anti-establishment as he was, Behan was not too proud to wish for the recognition of having his play produced by this world-renowned Irish theater. On the night *The Quare Fellow* opened at the Abbey, Behan, proudly resplendent in full dress, attended the play with his parents. He had finally achieved at least a qualified acceptance in his native city, even though his play entered Ireland via London. Ironically, when *The Quare Fellow* was produced by the Abbey, the company was occupying temporary quarters in the Queen's Theatre, which had at one time been leased by P. J. Bourke, Behan's uncle, and which Behan had frequented in his youth.

The next important production of *The Quare Fellow* was in November, 1958, when it opened off Broadway at the Circle-in-the-Square. Behan did not attend this opening night, for he felt that he must get on with the writing of his novel *the catacombs*— one of the last times he was able to turn down a public appearance in favor of concentrating on his work. This production of *The Quare Fellow* received mixed reviews. Judith Crist in the *Herald Tribune* called the play "little more than 'The Last Mile' with a brogue—and the inevitable Irish tenor singing mournfully offstage." [6] Brooks Atkinson of the *Times*, while noting the technical uncertainty of the play, gave it a generally good review:

At last Brendan Behan's "The Quare Fellow" has reached the stage of The Circle-in-the-Square, where it opened last evening. It turns out to be have been worth waiting for. A loose, sprawling, loquacious play, it is redeemed by the grimness of its subject, by the intimacy of the author's knowledge of the strange dark manners of prison life and by the rude exuberance of the dialogue. . . . He has a virtually unique knowledge of men shut away from society and the abnormal pressures that surround them. Best of all, he has a robust sense of independence. No one has tamed him yet. And his "comedy drama" as he labels it, is original, boisterous, and perceptive. Beyond the petty affairs of his people, he is aware of an impersonal authority that beggars all.[7]

The *Quare Fellow* had several other notable productions, including the television version of the play which was broadcast by B.B.C. on the night of November 5, 1958, with the theme "That Old Triangle" sung by Dominic Behan. In March, 1959, *The Quare Fellow* was presented in West Berlin, but was not a success; nor was Behan, who had gone to Germany for opening night. He gave one of the public performances he thought was expected of him, but the Germans were not amused.

In 1961 the film version of *The Quare Fellow* opened at the Rialto Theatre in London's Leicester Square. The film was directed by Arthur Dreifus, who had intended that Behan prepare the film script. When Behan did not complete it, the task fell to Dreifus, who changed Behan's play considerably. Warder Crimmin's part, which was played by the fine Irish actor Patrick McGoohan, was considerably expanded. The "quare fellow" was given a wife, and a love interest between Crimmin and the condemned man's wife was added. Thus, although the film was a fairly good one,[8] it bore little resemblance to the play Behan had written.

An excellent recording of *The Quare Fellow* has been made. Directed by Micheal O'hAodha of Radio Éireann and employing a talented cast of regular Radio Éireann performers, the recording communicates Behan's theme almost as well as does a stage production.

II *The Structure of* The Quare Fellow

The Quare Fellow has often been damned because of its loose, sprawling structure. Theatrical purists abhor the fact that the plot does not lend itself easily to traditional analysis. Essentially, the plot possesses no "complication," in the structural sense of the thickening of the plot, the buildup to the climax. And, if the structural "climax" of a play is the point at which the crucial question or conflict of the play must be resolved, *The Quare Fellow* has no climax. The basic question which the play poses is more overwhelming at the end of the play than at the beginning. The structure of the play, however, is relevant to its theme.

Behan is working for the same effect in *The Quare Fellow* as is Beckett in *Waiting for Godot* and Ionesco in *The Bald Soprano*. That is, Behan creates an imaginary world with no discernible cause-and-effect relationships in order to reflect the formlessness of contemporary experience. Ihab Hassan, in his excellent book *Radical Innocence*, notes that, in a world in which chance and absurdity rule human actions, the pattern of fiction "recognizes disorder—gratuitous actions, demonic intrusions, obsessive motives. The form reflects the inward darkness of things. . . . The very idea of causality is carried to a depth of causelessness." [9] And

Elizabeth Hardwick, in a recent essay in the *New York Review of Books,* states:

George Eliot said that she wrote her novels out of the belief in "the orderly sequence by which the seed brings forth a crop of its kind." We all have a nostalgia and longing for this order because it has been the heart of European fiction and drama. Incident after incident, each growing out of the other, united in a chain of significant motivation, of cause and effect—moments of human destiny strung out like beads on a string. This is what we mean, perhaps, when we say we "understand" a work of literary art. Yet each decade brings us the conviction that this order is no longer present to the serious writer. . . . Connections in fiction and also in drama have become like those of poetry. Tone and style hold the work together, create whatever emotional effect it will have upon us.[10]

Behan could construct a complex plot in the best nineteenth-century tradition, as his novel *The Scarperer* indicates. In neither *The Quare Fellow* nor *The Hostage* did he create such a plot, for it would have contradicted the theme he wished to assert.

The Quare Fellow has also been criticized for being "melodramatic." None of the characters are very well developed; they tend to be types; and it is not difficult to discern which ones are to be admired and which not. Since the characters are not well developed, none of them possess any very obvious internal motivation; for the source for the action of the play resides in the situation. The appeal to sentiment is also rather obvious. *The Quare Fellow* is, then, by most definitions, "melodramatic."

It is unfair, however, to equate the melodramatic with the esthetically inferior. If melodrama indeed is a separate genre, its unique qualities should not necessarily condemn it. Criticism of the drama, unfortunately, has tended to limit itself by the illogical assumption that tragedy is the highest form of theatrical art. In his persuasive article "Melodrama," James L. Rosenberg discusses this absurd game of ranking:

Why must generic classification necessarily degenerate into a game of hierarchies? Is it not enough to perceive that there are various modes of perception—the tragic, the comic, the melodramatic, the farcical, the pastoral, the epic? . . . Tragedy is certainly "different from" melodrama; this fact does not necessarily make it "better than." Can we not be satisfied with saying that tragedy and comedy and melodrama and farce are different modes of perception, each with its own validity, none necessarily better or worse than the others? [11]

Rosenberg also presents an excellent argument justifying the sensational aspects of melodrama: "We go to the theatre (as we do to the church, the athletic arena, the social center) to be made more aware of our aliveness. . . . There, everything matters; every moment is significant; nothing is wasted; there, life *really* burns with a hard gemlike flame—as it so rarely does on the other side of the footlights." [12] If one believes Rosenberg and Hassan, *The Quare Fellow* cannot be condemned merely because it represents a general type of drama which is by definition inferior. If one wants to prove the play inferior and inconsequential, he must make a close analysis of the play, a task most of those who have written on Behan have declined.

III   *Critical Analysis of* The Quare Fellow

The Quare Fellow, set in an Irish prison on the eve of an execution, is a direct result of Behan's experiences during his prison years. In *Confessions of an Irish Rebel*, he in fact relates the exact incident which inspired the play:

"Being summer, I had come in late from the exercising yard after a game of hand-ball with a young fellow from Limerick called Hickey . . . On this day as Hickey and I came in together, Bernard Kirwan was with his visitors and two warders, and shoving aside the two warders who stood aghast at the idea of a condemned man having contact with anybody, he dashed out from the cell and he embraced us both. . . . Years later I based my play 'The Quare Fellow' on the last few weeks of this man's life." [13]

The Quare Fellow is not, however, simply a reportorial account of Bernard Kirwan's last weeks and execution. It is Behan's unique, tragi-comic observation of man's schizoid nature—his capacity for evil, and his bent for kindness. As Kenneth Tynan noted in his review of *The Quare Fellow*, "Behan's convicts behave with hair-raising jocularity, exchanging obscene insults even while they are digging the murderer's grave. . . . With superb dramatic tact, the tragedy is concealed beneath layer after layer of rough comedy." [14] Tynan was not alone in sensing the unorthodox tone of the play. John Russell Taylor, in *Anger and After*, states that

"In *The Quare Fellow* the tragic undertones are always present, and though they are seldom insisted on we are conscious throughout of a sensation in the comedy akin to that of dancing on a coffin-lid." [15] Such dancing may be exactly what Behan had in mind in *The Quare Fellow,* and Behan comes by this propensity naturally, for this sort of behavior is an integral part of the time-honored Irish wake. Says Vivian Mercier, in *The Irish Comic Tradition,*

The Irish propensity for macabre humour may easily be traced to the world-renowned Irish wakes, at which merriment alternates with or triumphs over mourning, in the very presence of the corpse. Convivial drinking and cheerful conversation are the best-known features of modern wakes, but it is generally accepted that dancing, singing, and horse-play formed an essential part of the wakes in earlier times. Few people nowadays, even in Ireland, are aware that the old horse-play included some quite elaborate mimed dramas, reminiscent of fertility ritual. Lady Wilde went so far as to write "The Wake Orgies," while Henry Morris believed that the wake games "came down in unbroken descent through all the centuries from the Cluichthe Caointe, or 'Games of Lamentation,' mentioned so frequently in our pagan Irish literature." The similarity between the ancient Irish games and the funeral games so familiar in Homer has often been pointed out. In *A Handbook of Irish Folklore* Mr. Seán Ó Súlleabháin lists 130 specific wake games, besides a number of more informal wake amusements; among the latter we find "performing tricks on the corpse," a practice which might be the cause or effect of a macabre sense of humour but clearly has ritual status also.[16]

Obviously, however, many critics do not understand this comic-macabre aspect of *The Quare Fellow.* Judith Crist sees the play as a rather shallow bit of propaganda directed largely toward the evils of capital punishment: "No one says anything that has not been said in dozens of other prison dramas . . . there is little comedy and less drama on the stage." [17] In his objection to *The Quare Fellow* Richard Hayes asserts that "Capital punishment . . . is at once too proximate and too remote to provoke us to responses other than luxurious indignation or sadistic curiosity." [18]

The Quare Fellow is, however, much more than a humorous diatribe against capital punishment. Certainly, by the time the curtain drops on this "comedy-drama," the viewer is aware that

Behan is against the death penalty—as what ex-prisoner might not be. But *The Quare Fellow* is only incidentally an indictment of capital punishment. The play transcends any specific human cruelty. It is essentially a satire and a celebration—a satire on man's stupidity and a celebration of man's irrepressible vitality.

The prisoners of Behan's *The Quare Fellow* simply refuse to accept the stamp of inhumanity which a frightened society has tried to force upon them. If logic alone dictated the prisoners' actions, they should act in a gloomy, animalistic way—should become the lifeless ciphers that society has tried to make them. But these prisoners still retain their humanity, and the immense gap between what society's inhuman logic would attempt to make of these men and what they actually are leads to that incongruity which is an essential element of the comic. The assertion of man's vitality—his fundamental endurance—is evident throughout the play. It is perhaps most evident in Act III when the hanging is imminent, but even in Acts I and II, this human vitality refuses to be denied.

IV   Act I

The opening scene of the play sets the mood: "On the wall and facing the audience is printed in large block shaded Victorian lettering the word 'SILENCE'" (1),[19] but a prisoner in a punishment cell is singing a slightly off-color song to a plaintive tune:

> A hungry feeling came o'er me stealing,
> And the mice were squealing in my prison cell,
> And that old triangle
> Went jingle jangle
> Along the banks of the Royal Canal.
> (1)

The first action of the warder is to demand that he shut up; the first action of the prisoners who immediately appear from their cells is to attempt to laugh at their situation:

PRISONER A: Nice day for the races.
PRISONER B: Don't think I can make it. Too much to do at the office.
(2)

The joke is trite, but its freshness or humor is not important. The attempt to laugh as an assertion of vitality is. Then, the young prisoner begins singing again:

> There are hands that will welcome you in
> There are lips that I am burning to kiss
> There are two eyes that shine . . .
>
> . . . .
>
> Far away where the blue shadows fall
> I will come to contentment and rest,
> And the toils of the day
> Will all be charmed away . . .
>   (3)

As the song trails off, the old prisoner Dunlavin "appears in the cell polishing a large enamel chamber pot with a cloth" (3). The audience probably does not laugh until Dunlavin appears with the chamber pot; but Dunlavin's pot, though it obviously calls more immediate attention to itself, is like the lewd-sentimental song the young prisoner is singing—an affirmation of man's vitality in the face of a system which assumes punishment of the criminal to be more important than the wrongdoer's humanity. Behan simply, if rather crudely, is asking, "Do dead men need chamber pots?; Do dead men sing of love?; Can prison stifle the human spirit?"

This assertion of man's indomitable spirit is also apparent in the speech in which Dunlavin bemusedly and resignedly awaits the visit of "Holy Healy," a do-gooder with whom he hopes to curry favor. Dunlavin states: "I've got to hang up my holy pictures and think up a few funny remarks for him. God, what Jimmy O'Dea is getting thousands for I've to do for a pair of old socks and a ticket for the Prisoners' Aid" (9). Dunlavin simply will not capitulate. He is forced into playing the hypocrite, but he will not roll over and play dead.

Also attesting to the vitality of these imprisoned men is their propensity for those two elements—women and alcohol—which men anywhere are interested in as long as they draw the breath of life. Although the prisoners' ability to obtain either a woman or a drink is considerably limited, lack of availability has not dimmed the men's enthusiasm. Across the courtyard the men watch as the women prisoners hang up their washing:

DUNLAVIN: Women.

PRISONER A: I see the blondy one waving.

YOUNG PRISONER 1: If it's all the one to you, I'd like you to know that's my mot and it's me she's waving at.

. . . .

NEIGHBOR: What, are they gone in already?

DUNLAVIN: No, but they're finished hanging up the top row of clothes. There'll be no stretching or reaching off chairs.

NEIGHBOR: Still, thanks be to God for small mercies. They'll be out again this day week.   (16–17)

Although the contact with the "mots" is limited to merely looking, as is that of many a man not so confined as these, the drinking is not such a problem. Dunlavin and Neighbor, the old experienced prisoners, take advantage of softhearted Warder Regan; while he is rubbing their legs to relieve their pains of "rheumatism," the men drink long and deeply of the "methylated spirits" Regan is using. They expect to suffer from drinking the raw spirits. They even anticipate the hangover with detailed memories of previous suffering:

DUNLAVIN: . . . you'd fall down and sleep on the pavement of a winter's night and not know but you were lying snug and comfortable in the Shelbourne.

NEIGHBOR: Only then to wake up on some lobby and the hard floorboards under you, and a lump of hard filth for your pillow, and the cold and the drink shaking you, wishing it was morning for the market pubs to open, where if you had the price of a drink you could sit in the warm anyway. Except, God look down on you, if it was Sunday.

DUNLAVIN: Ah, there's the agony. No pub open, but the bells battering your bared nerves and all you could do with the cold and the sickness was to lean over on your side and wish that God would call you.   (22–23)

The essentially vital qualities of these men—the great life force apparent in spite of their life-destroying situation—is one of the major characteristics of Behan's comic technique. Behan's prisoners sing, they laugh, they drink, they admire women, they make trite off-color remarks (Neighbor: "The vet's here"; Dunlavin: "Hey, come out and get gelded [23].") But still there is a bit of a

desperate quality which becomes more and more evident as the
hanging comes closer and closer.

The second major characteristic of comedy evident in Behan's
The Quare Fellow is the play's satire. Even in prison, Behan indicates, man is the slave of foolish, irrational impulses which make
him less than he should be. Two of the prime examples of Behan's
satire on this human failing occur very early in the play. The two
prisoners under discussion in the following lines are the "quare
fellow"—the one to be hanged—and another murderer, the one
who was reprieved:

DUNLAVIN: The fellow beat his wife to death with the silver-topped
cane, that was a presentation to him from the Combined Staffs, Excess
and Refunds branch of the late Great Southern Railways, was reprieved, though why him any more than the other fellow is more nor
I can tell.

PRISONER A: Well, I suppose they looked at it, he only killed her
and left it at that. He didn't cut the corpse up afterwards with a butcher's knife.

DUNLAVIN: Yes, and then of course the other fellow used a meat-
chopper. Real bog-man act. Nearly as bad as a shotgun, or getting the
weed-killer mixed up in the stirabout. But a man with a silver-topped
cane, that's a cut above meat-choppers whichever way you look at it.
(4)

Somehow, either by not exercising reason, or by being influenced
by economic considerations, the officers of society have chosen to
give one man a reprieve and to hang the other. Both victims are
dead, and the fact that the body of one of them was mutilated
after the murder should really have no bearing on the case, unless,
as man in society vehemently denies, he possibly holds a higher
regard for the body than the spirit. Behan points out this incon-
sistency.

Nor are the prisoners themselves more sensible in their application of the notion of crime and punishment than the society outside the prison walls. The prisoners are happy with their murderer-
neighbor—"killing your wife is a natural class of thing could happen to the best of us" (5)—but they are extremely distressed to
find that their other new neighbor is "a bloody sex mechanic"
(24)—"They must think this is the bloody sloblands" (4). According to Dunlavin, "a new chap that's never done anything but mur-

der, and that only once, is usually a respectable man. . . . Bad
and all as Silver-Top was to beat his wife's brains out, I'd as lief
have him near to me as this article. Dirty beast! I won't have an
hour's luck for the rest of me six months . . ." (7–8).

Behan's satire on the manner in which the prisoners classify one
another is concluded with Dunlavin's statement after both prisoners have moved in: "God knows I got the pick of good neighbors.
Lovely people. Give me a decent murderer, though, rather than
the likes of this other fellow" (13). With Dunlavin's reference to
the assortment of cheats, thieves, robbers, and murderers gathered in this microcosmic world as "lovely people," Behan is satirically reminding us that the perversion of man's mind, which
in outside society rates a sexual lawbreaker lower than a murderer, does the same within the prison. Men are stupid, illogical, laughable, says Behan.

Another satiric point made in Act I is that in or out of prison,
youth is often shallow and unknowing:

YOUNG PRISONER 1: I suppose when you get old, though, you don't
much bother about women.

YOUNG PRISONER 2: I'm thirty-six, Mac.

YOUNG PRISONER 1: Ah, I thought that. Don't suppose you care if
you ever see a mot. (16)

The young prisoners, however, are in some areas respectful of
their elders:

YOUNG PRISONER 2: Do you think Triplex or celluloid is best for Yale
locks, sir?

YOUNG PRISONER 1: Do you carry the stick all the time, sir? (10)

Religion is another element which comes in for satiric treatment
in Act I. The most obvious target is Holy Healey, the Justice Department man who is "in some holy crowd that does good by
stealth. They never let the right hand know what the left hand
doeth, as the man said" (8). The Bible is also satirized—"As it
says in the Bible, sir, have it yourself or be without it and put ye
by for a rainy day, for thou knowest not the night thou mayest be
sleeping in a lobby" (31). The irrelevance of the Bible to the
everyday experiences of the prisoners is pointed out, for it must be

rewritten to comfort these men. Thus, the religious superstructure which man has erected to comfort the sinner becomes laughable. But Behan's prisoners do derive some comfort from the Bible:

NEIGHBOR: Many's the time the Bible was a consolation to a fellow all alone in the old cell. The lovely thin paper with a bit of mattress coir in it, if you could get a light, was as good a smoke as ever I tasted. Am I right, Dunlavin?

DUNLAVIN: Damn the lie, Neighbor. The first twelve months I done, I smoked my way half-way through the book of Genesis and three inches of my mattress. When the Free State came in we were afraid of our life they were going to change the mattresses for feather beds. And you couldn't smoke feathers, not, be God, if they were rolled in the Song of Solomon itself. (21)

Near the end of Act I, Silver-Top attempts to hang himself, for he is apparently unpersuaded that "life is a whole lot better than death any day of the week." This ironically violent action runs counter to the generally light tone which has prevailed in the first act, yet the juxtaposition of the violent and the serious with the playful and the comic is thematically relevant—as much so as the drunken porter in *Macbeth*. The horror of what Macbeth and his wife had done is heightened by contrast with the porter's drunken exuberance. The horror of any human death, whether exacted by society or by the victim's own hand, is forcefully asserted by Silver-Top's attempt to kill himself at the peak of that series of bursts of laughter which is Act I of *The Quare Fellow*. It is ironic and absurd that the man who has received no reprieve would give anything for another day of life and that the man who has been reprieved and sentenced to life attempts to carry out his own execution.

V *Act II*

Act II opens with another verse of "The Old Triangle." The prisoners are enjoying their evening exercise in the prison yard. In plain sight of all the prisoners is the half-dug grave which awaits the "quare fellow." Despite the morbidity of the situation and the setting, the atmosphere, which one would expect to be gloomy, is almost flippant. The prisoners, while obviously becoming more tense as the time of the hanging nears, nevertheless continue to assert their aliveness in the face of death. The prisoners look forward to the job of finishing the grave digging, rather than dreading the contact with the impending death; for it is an opportunity for a "couple of smokes"—a break in the monotony of prison life. Instead of avoiding the open grave, as one might expect, the prisoners make it an object of their jokes and jibes.

When one of the digging crew suddenly straightens up in the bottom of the grave, another prisoner comments wryly: "The dead arose and appeared to many" (55). Neighbor comments cheerfully: "A comfortable old flowery dell he'll have down there. We'll be eating cabbages off that one in a month or two" (37). Only the new prisoner finds the subject of hanging distasteful to him—obviously he has not acquired the hard shell required of a "tough con." In deference to him, the other prisoners understandingly wait until he is gone to "have a chat about it in peace" (38). The entire subject of the open grave is treated in such a manner that Regan is forced to reprimand the work crew: "I've been watching you for the last ten minutes and damn the thing you've done except yap, yap, yap the whole time. The Chief or the Governor or any of them could have been watching you. They'd have thought it was a bloody mothers' meeting" (59–60).

Throughout this act, Dunlavin, as expected, suffers from the aftereffects of drinking the rubbing alcohol—a situation which he fully expected and which occupies his mind to the exclusion of thoughts of the "quare fellow":

NEIGHBOR: How are you, Neighbor?
DUNLAVIN: Dying
NEIGHBOR: If you are itself, it's greed that's killing you. I only got a sup of what was left.
DUNLAVIN: I saved your life then; it was very bad meths.
PRISONER: What did Regan say when he caught youse lying in the cell?
NEIGHBOR: He wanted to take us up for drinking it on him, but Dunlavin said we were distracted with the events of the morning and didn't know what we were doing. So he just told us to get to hell out of it and he hoped it would destroy us for life.
DUNLAVIN: May God forgive him.
NEIGHBOR: I thought it was as good a drop of meths as ever I tasted. It would never come up to the pre-war article, but between the springtime and the warmth of it, it would put new life into you.   (35–36)

Again the vitality in the hearts of these men keeps them from the gloom and discouragement which could so easily be theirs, even if part of that vitality comes out of a bottle.

As Act II progresses, however, the terror and desperation which the men feel as the hanging approaches again and again break through the surface of their rough humor. Behan's satiric thrusts also become more pointed, and near the end of the act he substitutes direct statement for satire. Just after the hangman arrives, the kindly Warder Regan states, with rather embarrassing naïveté and obviousness, that a corrupt society is to blame for capital punishment. Luckily, however, Behan limits these intrusive direct comments, and Act II ends with a bitterly ironic comment by Warder Regan concerning the official instructions for the treatment of a condemned prisoner: "As the old Home office memorandum says, 'An air of cheerful decorum is indicated, as a readiness to play such games as draughts or luco, or snakes and ladders; a readiness to enter into conversations on sporting topics will also be appreciated'" (66).

VI *Act III*

Both scenes of Act III of *The Quare Fellow* are characterized by the bitterness of their satire. A man is to be hanged, yet those in charge of this legalized murder concern themselves only with the most petty affairs. The incongruity between what these characters, as human beings, should be concerning themselves with and what they actually concern themselves with produces some rather "black comedy," which must make the audience uncomfortable, even as it laughs.

Early in the first scene of Act III, two warders are discussing their careers, and the fact that a hanging is imminent does not seem to bother them. Warder 1 tells Warder 2: "We're in it for the three P's, boy, pay, promotion and pension, that's all that should bother civil servants like us" (68). Warder 1 wishes to be promoted, and he is obviously cultivating the support of the acquiescent Warder 2. What are the rewards for the junior Warder? Warder 1 spells it out for him: "Don't be surprised if you get your landing sooner than you expected. Thirty cells all to yourself before you're fifty" (71). Certainly, Behan is not satirizing for its own sake the wish of any man to achieve some sort of success. He is, however, satirizing the desire to get ahead inasmuch as that desire makes man ignore the plight of his fellow human beings. In their concern with getting and gaining, the two warders have no sensitivity at all to normal human values—a lack perhaps most evident in their discussion of the prison Canon:

> WARDER 1: He was silenced for something before he came here and this is the *only* job he can get. Something terrible he did, though God forgive us, maybe it's not right to talk of it.
> WARDER 2: You might sing it.
> WARDER 1: I hear it was the way that he made the housekeeper take a girl into the house, the priest's house, to have a baby, an illegitimate!
> WARDER 2: And could a man like that be fit to be a priest!
> WARDER 1: He'd hardly be fit to be a prison chaplain, even. (70–71)

Obviously, the priest's action was a foolish one if judged by the inhuman logic of personal gain, and this sort of selfish pushing Behan attacks throughout *The Quare Fellow*.

How far out of joint the affairs of this microcosmic society are is satirized perhaps most bitterly in the treatment which Behan gives to the hangman. It seems the hangman, though he travels the countryside executing people, has his own problems. When a prisoner on the hangman's last visit stole part of the hangman's breakfast, the Chief and the Governor were quite concerned:

> CHIEF: Last time they were here, some hungry pig ate half his breakfast and he kicked up murder.
> GOVERNOR: See it doesn't happen this time.
> CHIEF: No indeed. There's a fellow under sentence of death next week in the Crumlin; we don't want him going up to Belfast and saying we starved him. (73)

Though the "quare fellow" is still alive, the deafening noise of the falling trap echoes in the mind of the audience. The fact that the Chief and the Governor cannot hear this echo is bitterly ironic. They are no longer human; they have become cogs in a murderous machine, unfeeling men who are more concerned with a strip of bacon than with a man's life.

Everything must go according to plan. The hanging must not be delayed by any mixup such as the one which had occurred before an earlier hanging when the hangman got drunk:

CHIEF: Once he went straight from the boat to the pubs and spent
the day in them, and when he got here wasn't he after leaving the
black box with his rope and his washers and his other little odds and
ends behind him in a pub and forgot which one it was he left them in.
GOVERNOR: Really.
CHIEF: You could sing it. You were in Limerick at the time, sir, but
here we were, in a desperate state. An execution coming off in the
morning and we without the black box that had all his tools in it. The
Governor we had then, he promised a novena to St. Anthony and two
insertions in the *Messenger* if they were found in time. And sure enough
after squad cars were all over in the city, the box was got in a pub
down the North Wall, the first one he went into. It shows you the power
of prayer, sir.   (73–74)

Ritual, order, and tidiness are the shallow gods of the Chief and
the Governor, who, after all, are only representative of the society
which employs them. The fact that a human being should be sad-
dened at the death of a fellow human being is quite obvious—the
fact that the Chief and the Governor are not properly concerned
is equally obvious. The vast gap between what these men should
feel and what they do feel (and the audience must to some extent
see itself in the Chief and the Governor) must cause a bitter, almost humorless sort of laughter.

The Governor's failure to realize the horror that he and his un-
derlings are about to commit is again underlined in this first scene
of the third act. The Governor has been to dinner at his School
Union and is outraged at the attitude he found there:

GOVERNOR: Good God, this sort of thing is getting out of hand. I
was at my School Union this evening. I had to leave in sheer embarrass-
ment; supposedly witty remarks made to me at my own table. My el-
dest son was furious with me for going at all. He was at a table with a
crowd from the University. They were even worse. One young pup
went so far as to ask him if he thought I would oblige with a rendering
of "The night before Larry was stretched." I shall certainly tell the
Principal that there's at least one place in this city where an execution
is taken very seriously indeed.   (74–75)

The execution is indeed taken seriously inside the walls of the
prison, if one agrees that the petty details of the hanging are its
essence. If the essential fact of the hanging is that a man's life is to

be taken, it is quite clear that the Chief and the Governor take the execution with little more seriousness than do those on the outside, who scorn the death of the "quare fellow" by laughing at it. When Behan also laughs at the hanging, he is not laughing at the "quare fellow," but at the insensitive society carrying out the execution.

Behan's satire at times becomes obviously didactic in this act, and he seems so aroused that he no longer trusts the indirect devices of comedy. Midway through the first scene, for instance, Behan has Warder Regan, in a conversation with the Chief, directly attack the execution:

REGAN: And you're not going to give me that stuff about just shoving over the lever and bob's your uncle. You forget the times the fellow gets caught and has to be kicked off the edge of the trap hole. You never heard of the warders down below swinging on his legs the better to break his neck, or jumping on his back when the drop was too short.
CHIEF: Regan, I hope you'll forget those things you mentioned just now. If talk the like of that got outside the prison . . .
REGAN: I think the whole show should be put on in Croke Park; after all, it's at the public expense and they let it go on. They should have something more for their money than a bit of paper stuck up on the gate.   (76)

Behan's direct attack on capital punishment in particular and on inhuman insensitivity in general is soon, however, subsumed under a wave of biting satire. The hangman, because he drinks heavily before an execution and usually cannot find his way back to the prison without help, brings with him on each trip a man named Jenkinson as his keeper. Jenkinson is an evangelist, a teetotaler, and a hymn writer; and, while the hangman calculates the length of the drop which will break the "quare fellow's" neck, Jenkinson favors the audience with a song. This scene's satiric counterpoint is so masterfully done that it deserves full quotation:

JENKINSON: My brother, sit and think.
While yet some time is left to thee
Kneel to thy God who from thee does not shrink
And lay thy sins on Him who died for thee.
HANGMAN: Take a fourteen-stone man as a basis, and giving him a drop of eight foot . . .

JENKINSON: Men shrink from thee but not I,
                  Come close to me I love my erring sheep.
                  My blood can cleanse thy sins of blackest dye,
                  I understand if thou canst only weep.
HANGMAN: Every half-stone lighter would require a two-inch longer
drop, so for weight thirteen and a half stone—drop eight feet two
inches, and for weight thirteen stone—drop eight feet four inches.
JENKINSON: Though thou hast grieved me sore,
                  My arms of mercy still are open wide,
                  I still hold open Heaven's shining door
                  Come then, take refuge in my wounded side.
HANGMAN: Now he's only twelve stone so he should have eight foot
eight, but he's got a thick neck on him so I'd better give him another
couple of inches. Yes, eight foot ten.
JENKINSON: Come now, the time is short
                  Longing to pardon and bless I wait.
                  Look up to me, my sheep so dearly bought
                  And say, forgive me, ere it is too late.
HANGMAN: Divide 412 by the weight of the body in stones, multiply
by two gives the length of the drop in inches.   (79–80)

Again Behan has pointed his finger at the crass insensitivity of
human nature and especially at the irrelevance of a religion which
sings but does not sympathize.

Immediately following the horror which Behan realizes in the
Jenkinson-Hangman counterpoint, Warder Regan speaks directly
and sentimentally against capital punishment: "Thanks for the
hymn. Great night for stars. If there's life on any of them, I wonder do the same things happen up there? Maybe some warders on
a planet are walking across a prison yard this minute and some
fellow up there waiting on the rope in the morning, and looking
out through the bars, for a last look at our earth and the moon for
the last time. Though I never saw them to bother much about
things like that. It's nearly always letters to their wives or mothers,
and then we don't send them—only throw them into the grave
after them. What'd be the sense of broadcasting such distressful
rubbish?" (81).

But lest Regan's argument become overly sentimental, Behan
initiates another life-death counterpoint. Prisoner C sings from his
cell window, "Is e fath mo bhuadhartha na bhaghaim cead curts."
(It is the cause of my sorrow that I have not permission to visit

[81]). He's singing for the "quare fellow," says Regan. When
Crimmin asks why the Hangman wanted to know if the "quare
fellow" was a Catholic, Regan replies, "So as they'd know to have
the hood slit to anoint him on the rope, and so as the fellows below would know to take off his boots and socks for the holy oil on
his feet when he goes down" (81). The singing of Prisoner C a-
gain is heard: "N'il gaoth adtuaidh ann, N'il sneachta cruaidh
ann . . ." (There is no north wind there, there is no hard snow
there . . . [81]). "We'd better be getting in," says Regan. "The
other screws will be hopping mad to get out; they've been there
since four o'clock today" (81). And the song of Prioner C replies,
"Mo whuirnin bhan . . ." (My white darling mavourneen [81]).
Again Behan has established the primary tension of the play—the
conflict between the death-dealing ritual of society and the life-
affirming cry of the solitary human being.

The last scene of the third act deals with the actual moment of
the execution, the digging of the grave, and the carving into the
prison wall of the "quare fellow's" only memorial—his prison
number. At this point in the play, as the death of the "quare fellow" grows nearer and nearer, it is quite obvious that the comedy
which affirms man's vitality is almost completely absent. The tone
is somber and dark, and the prison is astir with an animal tension.
Yet, even in this last sordid hour, the human beings of this microcosmic world refuse to give the grave a complete victory. The
prisoners, in turning the "quare fellow's" "last mile" into a sort of
horse race, refuse to accept, as have the Governor and the Chief
before them, the basic fact of the "quare fellow's" death; the prisoners' turning his last steps into a race, however, is born not of
indifference but of sympathy. They attempt to laugh because the
weeping would be too painful:

MICKSER: We're ready for the start, and in good time and who do I
see lined up for the off but the High Sheriff of this ancient city of ours,
famous in song and story as the place where the pig ate the whitewash
brushes and—We're off, in this order: The Governor, the Chief, two
screws Regan and Crimmin, the quare fellow between them, two more
screws and three runners from across the Channel, getting well in front,
now the Canon. He's making a big effort for the last two furlongs. He's
got the white pudding bag on his head, just a short distance to go.
He's in.   (82)

But at the last, as the "quare fellow" dies, the prisoners can no longer articulate their sympathy through laughter and they cry out as would a wounded animal: (*"The hour strikes. The Warders cross themselves and put on their caps. From the Prisoners comes a ferocious howling."* [83]). All that is left now is to bury the "quare fellow" and to carve in the stone wall the dead man's registration number:

> CHIEF: Yes, that's it. You're to carve E. 777. Got that?
> PRISONER B: Yes, sir. E. 777.
> CHIEF: That's it. It should be E. 779 according to the book, but a "7" is easier for you to do than a "9". Right, the stone on the wall that's nearest to the spot. Go ahead now. There's the usual two bottles of stout a man, but only if you work fast.   (85)

Even the "quare fellow's" anonymity is not sacred. He has become even less than a mere number, and Behan's satire has become so bitter that there is little possibility of laughter.

Just before the closing curtain, the convicts, who have been relatively on the side of virtue throughout the play, are subjected to some of Behan's most vicious satire. The "quare fellow" has written several letters home during his time on death row. As has been noted, it is the custom of the prison not to deliver these letters. However, the prisoners on the burying detail realize the sensational and monetary value which the "quare fellow's" letters would have if they could be smuggled out and published in the Sunday press. So, even before the "quare fellow" has been properly laid to rest, his fellow prisoners engage in a sad and vicious argument over his letters:

> PRISONER A: Give us them bloody letters. They're worth money to one of the Sunday papers.
> PRISONER B: So I understood you to say yesterday.
> PRISONER A: Well, give us them.
> PRISONER D: They're not exclusively your property any more than anyone else's.
> PRISONER B: There's no need to have a battle over them. Divide them. Anyone that likes can have my share and I suppose the same goes for the kid.
> PRISONER D: Yes, we can act like businessmen. There are three. One each and toss for the third. I'm a businessman.   (86)

No more than the soldiers who gambled for Christ's robe do the prisoners realize the horror of what they are doing. Behan and his audience do realize the coarse inhumanity of the convicts; yet Behan's bitterest satire is never misanthropic. *The Quare Fellow,* Behan's comment on man's inhumanity to man, has a sad and serious theme. But no one who sees or reads this play can ignore the basic fact that it is on the side of life.

The Quare Fellow has its weaknesses—this cannot be denied; but its strength lies in its vitality—its affirmation of life. Indeed, if this is a funeral, or a wake, Behan is asking us not only to mourn but to hope; "to laugh and shout and sing, as well as to weep and wail and shudder." [20] Behan called the play a "comedy-drama." In *La Petite Molière* Jean Anouilh defines this type of play very well: "Certainly everything is ugly, everything is sad, and afterwards we know it. But the soul must be purged by laughter. The only virile attitude to take in the face of the human condition is to laugh at it. And that is comedy."

CHAPTER 4

The Hostage

I've always thought T. S. Eliot wasn't far wrong when he said that the main problem of the dramatist today is to keep his audience amused; and that while they were laughing their heads off, you could be up to any bloody thing behind their backs; and it was what you were doing behind their bloody backs that made your play great.

—*Brendan Behan's Island*

I *Stage History*

BEHAN'S second play *An Giall* was commissioned by the Irish language organization Gael Linn and was produced in Dublin's Damer Hall in June, 1958. The play had a routine run and apparently offended none of the Dubliners who viewed it, probably because very few of them could understand Irish well enough to be aware of the bitterness with which Behan was attacking Irish shibboleths. Subsequent Dublin productions of *An Giall* in its English form, *The Hostage*, were not so quietly received.

Behan claimed to have written the Irish-language version of his play in twelve days. This claim appears, however, to have been another of Behan's attempts to make the public believe that he did his work with little effort and very little care. The recollection of Riobaird MacGabhrain, manager of Gael Linn, is that the play trickled in bit by bit, each payment by him bringing another installment from Behan.[1] In a September 30, 1957, letter to Iain Hamilton of Hutchison, Behan says he is writing *An Giall;*[2] and the evidence indicates that he had not yet completed the play by January, 1958, when he and Beatrice traveled to Spain. In fact, the major part of *An Giall* was probably written on Ibiza. In any case, the play was clearly not written in twelve days.

On October 14, 1958, the first English-language production of *The Hostage* opened in Joan Littlewood's Theatre Workshop at the Theatre Royal, Stratford, London. The production was a near thing, for the Theatre Workshop was having financial difficulties, and Brendan Behan was not. As the money rolled in, Behan became increasingly dilatory; and he finished the translation of *The Hostage* only because Gerry Raffles, manager of the Workshop, virtually forced him to complete the project.[3]

The reviewers were generally good to *The Hostage,* though few of them were able to discern its theme and most seemed to be so carried along by the raucous byplay that they neglected to examine it in much depth. The *London Times* review, an excellent example, overemphasizes the topical at the expense of delving into the meaning of the play. To the *Times* the play was a hilarious account of things Anglo-Irish: *The Hostage* "treats past and present Anglo-Irish relations with a laughing impartiality which is almost anarchic. . . . Behan understands the Cockney as well as he does his Irish types." [4]

In April, 1959, *The Hostage* was chosen to represent Great Britain at the *Theâtre des Nations* festival. Behan traveled to Paris for this production of the play, and both he and *The Hostage* were enthusiastically received. Behan could not, however, endure the adulation he received in France, and the binge in which he indulged on this trip exhausted him.

From the Theatre Workshop *The Hostage* moved to the West End, opening at Wyndham's Theatre on July 11, 1959. Behan was not on hand for the opening night, but he soon repaired this neglect by escaping from the hospital where he was being treated for alcoholism and by charging across the Irish Sea to give one of his classic drunken performances. Again the play proved to be of sturdier stuff than the man who created it. *The Hostage* was well received and was still on the boards long after Behan had returned to Dublin, having completely exhausted both the patience of the English police and his own body.

The next noteworthy production of *The Hostage* was on Broadway. On September 20, 1960, Behan's play opened at the Cort Theater, again under the direction of Joan Littlewood. Five of the seven reviewers for the New York papers praised *The Hostage.* Only John McClain of the *Journal American* failed to see anything of value in the play: "Mr. Behan, the author, has a certain gift for humor in the most disorderly sense, and no possible appreciation of play construction. The evening is a series of soiled vignettes, with atrocious language, no plausible point, and some of the funniest remarks you have heard late and loaded in 3rd avenue saloons." [5] But, he concluded, *The Hostage*, like the jokes one laughs at when drunk, was not so funny the next day.

The other critics, though noting that the play contained hardly anything traditional, were able to appreciate the thematic significance of the play's wild humor. *The Hostage*, according to Richard Watts of the *Post*, "is brimming with magnificent exuberance, wild unruly, scornful, satirical and mocking, filled with comic gusto and streaked through with an oddly embarrassed compassion. A kind of savagely disorderly vaudeville show, it throbs with sardonic vitality and an instinct for dramatic richness." Frank Aston of the *World Telegram* noted that before *The Hostage* "has run its course it collides with most of the rules on playmaking but gallops right along without a tremor. As far as I am concerned, it is enchanting." Walter Kerr of the *Herald Tribune* perceptively wrote: "This is a serious play which has to do with the howling foolishness of bothering our heads over all our minor skirmishes and empty civil squabbles while the hydrogen bomb is waiting in the wings." Howard Taubman, though noting Behan's lack of discipline, said that he revealed "a flair for drama and a determination to communicate something." Justin Gilbert of the *Mirror* called *The Hostage* a "serio-comic morality show. . . . a whopping chunk of earthy entertainment."

The Hostage closed its first New York run January 7, 1961, having moved from the Cort to the Ethel Barrymore, and then to the Eugene O'Neill. The play was still drawing an audience sufficient to make an off-Broadway performance profitable, but difficulties with union rules would not permit such a move at this time. Approximately a year later the play was revived off-Broadway, but it was not to receive a fraction of the critical notice which it had enjoyed on Broadway, though in 1962 the prestigious French Theater Critical Association, Le Syndicat de la Critique Dramatique, chose *The Hostage* as the best play of the season.

Because of Behan's last five stumbling years, many theater critics have concluded that Behan was responsible for neither *The Quare Fellow* nor *The Hostage*, and that *The Hostage* especially was the creation of Joan Littlewood. It is also darkly whispered that Behan stole the plot for *The Hostage* from Frank O'Connor's short story, "The Guests of a Nation." The fact aside that Behan actually knew such a house as he described in *The Hostage*, the plot of *The Hostage* resembles that of "The Guests of a Nation" only in the vaguest way. In O'Connor's story, two old English soldiers, not one young one, are held hostage. O'Connor's story contains no love interest, and the two Englishmen are killed intentionally at the end and not by accident, as is Behan's Leslie. The vastly different tone of the two pieces would be in itself sufficient to absolve Behan of unacknowledged borrowing from O'Connor. That such a charge is made at all is merely another instance of that Irish literary jealousy which found it difficult to acknowledge that Brendan Behan had any talent.

II   The Hostage *as "Theatre of the Absurd"*

Martin Esslin, in *The Theatre of the Absurd,* convincingly argues that "absurdist drama" is the drama of quest and awareness:

In expressing the tragic sense of loss at the disappearance of ultimate certainties the Theatre of the Absurd, by a strange paradox, is also a symptom of what probably comes nearest to being a genuine religious quest in our age: an effort, however timid and tentative, to sing, to laugh, to weep—and to growl—if not in praise of God . . . at least in search of a dimension of the Ineffable; an effort to make man aware of the ultimate realities of his condition, to instill in him again the lost sense of cosmic wonder and primeval anguish, to shock him out of an existence that has become trite, mechanical, complacent, and deprived of the dignity that comes of awareness.[6]

Esslin does not mention Behan in *The Theatre of the Absurd,* but what Esslin has to say about such playwrights as Ionesco and Beckett clearly applies equally well to Behan. The outrageous humor and disconnected music-hall plot of *The Hostage* are most certainly designed to shock people out of their trite, mechanical, and complacent existence. Behan shows—as do Beckett, Ionesco, Pinter, and Genet—that man is ridiculous when he allows himself to be controlled by a system. In addition, Behan is in complete agreement with the other "absurdist" dramatists in realizing that, in spite of man's historical fascination with the ingenious manacles of inhumanity which he has forged for himself, the human being contains a vital animal spirit which can be stilled neither by man's own stupidity nor by the absurdity of the universe.

At the end of *Rhinoceros,* Ionesco's sad little hero Beranger, who has seen his friends metamorphize into something quite inhuman—a herd of rhinoceroses—shouts, "I'll take on the whole lot of them! I'll put up a fight against the lot of them, the whole lot of them! I'm the last man left, and I'm staying that way until the end. I'm not capitulating!" Beranger is fascinated by the inhuman, by the scaly green skins and virile horns of his friends; yet there exists in him a basic humanity which he cannot obliterate, even if he wants to. Behan's Leslie, who, after being shot, jumps up for a rousing chorus of "The bells of hell go ting-a-ling-a-ling," is saying in his song essentially the same thing that Beranger says in his last speech. The human spirit is indomitable. Neither the world nor man himself may destroy it.

As obvious as is Behan's agreement with the thematic assertions of the "Theatre of the Absurd," even more obvious is his employing in *The Hostage* the theatrical techniques of "absurdist drama." Esslin notes that the "Theatre of the Absurd" differentiates itself from traditional drama by emphasizing certain rather spectacular effects:

> The age-old traditions that the Theatre of the Absurd displays in new and individually varied combinations—and, of course, as the expression of wholly contemporary problems and preoccupations—might perhaps be classed under the headings of:
>
>> "Pure" theatre; i.e., abstract scenic effects
>> as they are familiar in the circus or review,
>> in the work of jugglers, acrobats, bullfighters,
>> or mimes.
>> Clowning, fooling, and mad-scenes.
>> Verbal nonsense.
>> The literature of dream and fantasy, which often has a
>> strong allegorical component.[7]

The Hostage qualifies on all four counts. The wild dances and seemingly irrelevant bits of song which *The Hostage* contains certainly could be called "pure" theater as well as "clowning." Monsewer plays one vast "mad scene," and he forces the other inhabitants of the brothel to play the scene with him. The "verbal nonsense" of *The Hostage* is all too obvious: "A 'brockel'—that's English for a whorehouse"; "Meanwhile I'll sing that famous old song, 'The Hound that Caught the Pubic Hare.'" An aura of "dream and fantasy" surrounds all of the events of *The Hostage*. The entire play seems a sort of mad hallucination of Ireland and the world gone mad, and Leslie's closing song adds another dimension of fantasy to the play.

To prove that *The Hostage* is an "absurdist drama" is important in that it serves at least partially to liberate Behan from the charge that *The Hostage* is a failure and that Behan was a man of no talent because his play breaks with nineteenth-century formulas of play construction. "Absurdist" dramatists eschew nineteenth-century traditions of plot and character presentation because they wish to show a chaotic world, one without logic or tradition. This is the world Behan wishes to show, and he chooses the techniques of "absurdist drama," not because of lack of talent, but because of his view of the world.

III *Act I*

In *The Hostage,* as in *The Quare Fellow,* Behan has created a microcosmic world; and many critics have noted that Behan's brothel bears certain resemblances to the frantic contemporary world. Harold Clurman notes that *"The Hostage* in its oblique, cockeyed, drunken eloquence . . . is finally a social play in the dizzy mode of 1960. It is the peeling that is coming off the walls of our decaying fortress." [8] Behan's brothel is a "noble old house" which has seen better days, housed many heroes, and is now "turned into a knocking shop" (105). It is, says Benedict Kiely, "romantic, idealistic Ireland fallen on sordid, materialistic days . . . heroic Ireland down in the dumps; it is the world in a mess." [9]

The Hostage also resembles *The Quare Fellow* in that it is practically plotless. An eighteen-year-old Irish boy has been sentenced to die in the Belfast jail for killing an Ulster policeman; while he awaits execution, the I.R.A. takes as hostage Leslie Williams, a young English soldier, lodges him in a brothel, and threatens to kill him if the Irish boy is executed. The Irish boy is executed by the English, and the English soldier is also killed, not by intention but by accident. In the short time Leslie spends in the brothel, he wins the sympathy of Pat, Meg, and obviously Teresa. It is clear that they will make every effort to spirit him out of the house before the I.R.A. can execute him. But, before Leslie can escape,

the police raid the brothel to rescue him. In the melee, Leslie is
killed. He springs up again, however; and, as the curtain falls, he
leads the cast in a last exuberant chorus of "The bells of hell go
ting-a-ling-a-ling."

The accidental nature of Leslie's death and his rising from the
dead are thematically significant, though critics have generally
been obtuse in understanding what Behan intends in so unexpectedly resurrecting Leslie. The important point, however, is that
both of Behan's major plays are finally concerned with death.
Whether Behan had the sheer writing talent of a Noel Coward
or a James Barrie, it is clear that his comic sense was never a
retreat from life. Never did Behan create a *Blithe Spirit* or a
Dear Brutus, and never did Behan use the comic as an excuse to
keep from looking at life.

Act I of *The Hostage* opens with the stage direction, *"Whole
company dances an Irish jig after two figures in which two whores
and two queers have danced together"* (91). These characters,
though they represent the most disreputable types of humanity,
play the game gaily and almost proudly. They are outcast, but
they are alive; and their raucous banter is an affirmation. Even
though the world does not want them, they have a capacity for
laughter—that ability which is finally the distinguishing characteristic of the human being:

> 1st WHORE: (to queers) Get off the stage, you dirty low things.
> COLETTE: A decent whore can't get a shilling round here for the likes
> of you.
> PRINCESS GRACE: To hell with you, and your friends in America.
> Come on dear, take no notice of them.
> 1st WHORE: Go get a mass said for yourself.
> PRINCESS GRACE: What we need round here is a bit of tolerance.
>
> (91)

The wild dance of those whom society has cuckolded lasts only
for a moment. At the instant the dance ends, the wild cacophonic
strains of Monsewer's bagpipes are heard offstage; and they an-
nounce the tragic theme of the play:

> MEG: In the name of God, what's that?
> PAT: It's only Monsewer practising his music. He has taken it into

his head to play the Dead March for the boy in Belfast Jail when they hang him in the morning.   (91)

Behan does not, however, allow contemplation of the tragic for long. As Meg and Pat discuss the boy in Belfast jail, Meg asks Pat if he thinks the English will really carry out the sentence. Says Pat, "There's no think about it. Tomorrow morning at the hour of eight, he'll hang as high as Killymanjaro." "What the hell's that?" says Meg. "A noted mountain off the south coast of Switzerland," comes the reply (92). This juxtaposition of the comic and tragic is typically Behan, for it is a major element in *The Quare Fellow* and *Borstal Boy* as well as in *The Hostage*.

Out of the tragic-comic tension of *The Hostage* the same sort of statement emerges as in *The Quare Fellow:* man is ridiculous; man is alive. Certainly the satiric impulse is obvious in *The Hostage,* most notably in the fun that Behan makes of Monsewer. Pat says, "It's bad enough for that old idiot not to have a clock, but I declare to Jesus, I don't think he even has a calendar. And who has all the trouble of it? I have. He wants to have the new I.R.A., so called, in this place now. 'Prepare a room for them,' no less. Bad enough running this place as a speak-easy and a brockel—" (92). In this house, as in O'Casey's tenement in *Juno and the Paycock,* the clock is on its face; and the past intrudes into and controls the present. When Pat is abused for his loyalty to Monsewer, he replies: "And who would look after him, in England or Ireland, if I didn't? I stick by him, because we were soldiers of Ireland in the old days" (93). But Monsewer and his anachronistic patriotism have served to turn the noble old house which housed so many heroes into a "knocking shop," for Pat simply cannot keep the house going on what Monsewer gives him.

The manner in which Monsewer became concerned in the fight for Irish independence is also satirized, for Monsewer's involvement seems more personal and accidental than sincerely patriotic:

PAT: He was born an Englishman and remained one for years . . . He had riches and every class of comfort you could wish for, till he found out he was an Irishman.
MEG: Aren't you after telling me he was an Englishman?
PAT: He was an Anglo-Irishman.
MEG: In the blessed name of God, what's that?
PAT: A Protestant with a horse.

MEG: And what do they do when they're out?

PAT: Well, an Anglo-Irishman only works at riding horses, you know, and drinking whisky, or reading double-meaning books in Irish at Trinity College.

MEG: I'm with you now; he wasn't born one, he became one.

PAT: He didn't become one—he was one—on his mother's side, and as he didn't like his father much he went with his mother's people—he became an Irishman.

MEG: How did he do that?

PAT: Well, there's not all that much difference. He started going to Irish classes in the Gaelic League in Red Lion Passage and wearing a kilt and playing Gaelic football in Blackheath, but then he threw the hammer after the hatchet and acted like a true Irishman here.

MEG: He came over to live in Ireland.

PAT: He fought for Ireland.   (101–02)

And, if the audience cannot understand these bitterly satiric comments on outworn Irish nationalism, Behan, through Pat, makes his attitude explicit: "This is nineteen-fifty-eight, and the days of the heroes is over this thirty-five years past. Long over, finished and done with. The I.R.A. and the War of Independence are as dead—as dead as the Charleston" (92). When the soldiers appear with the young English hostage, Pat is not afraid to speak his feelings plainly even to them:

PAT: . . . your real trouble when you go to prison as a patriot, do you know what it will be?

OFFICER: The loss of liberty.

PAT: No, the other Irish patriots, in along with you.   (117)

Behan satirizes many other aspects of Irish stupidity throughout *The Hostage*. In Act I, the subsidiary targets are religion and the Irish pretense to a national language. Both satires, however, are largely ineffectual because the butt for the satire in each case is rather flimsy. Miss Gilchrist, who represents the irrelevance and shallow piety of religion, explains that her name is "an old Irish name. In its original form 'Giolla Christ,' the servant or Gilly of Christ" (110). More "gilly" than servant is Miss Gilchrist. She spouts hymns at any provocation, accepts insults "in the name of our insulted saviour," constantly prays for and forgives the residents of the house. Behan's attitude toward Miss Gilchrist has caused many Catholic critics to cry "blasphemy"; but, rather than mocking belief, he is attacking the ridiculous posturing of the shallowly pious and the basic irrelevance of any sort of religious ritual when a man's life is at stake. The shame is that Miss Gilchrist is so obviously a straw woman that any argument Behan marshals against her is also bound to be straw.

The other obvious target for Behan's minor satiric thrust in Act I, the Irish language and the pride the Irish have in their Gaelic, points out the futility of nationalistic sentimentality:

PAT: When Monsewer came here, Meg, he wouldn't talk anything but Irish.

MEG: Most people wouldn't know what he was saying, surely.

PAT: They did not. When he went on a tram car or a bus he had to have an interpreter with him so as the conductor would know where he wanted to get off.   (99–100)

Behan's strange people live in a house and in a world which contains a good many subjects that cry out for satire. It seems, in fact, that Pat, Meg, Mulleady, Miss Gilchrist, Leslie, and Teresa have no reason at all to live; but they do live. In the face of all the stupidity which faces them—both their own and that imposed on them from outside—they exist. They not only live, but laugh. They may have been ground down incredibly near the animal level of existence, yet they do what no animal can do. They laugh, though this laughter seems often ritual and uninspired:

MONSEWER: For Ireland's sake I would hang crucified in the town square.

PAT: Let's hope it would be a fine day for you.

MEG: Or you wouldn't get the crowd.   (125)

. . . .

PAT: Is he a policeman?

TERESA: Oh no, sir, he looks respectable.

PAT: I can't see without my glasses. Has he a trench coat and a badge?

TERESA: The badge says he speaks only Irish.

PAT: Begod, then him and me would have to use the deaf and dumb language, for the only bit of Irish I can say would get us both prosecuted. That badge makes me think he's an officer.

MEG: An officer?

TERESA: He has another to say he doesn't drink.

PAT: That makes him a higher officer.   (113)

. . . .

OFFICER: May I see the toilet arrangements?

PAT: This *way*, sir. Mind your head as you go in.   (115)

IV *Act II*

Act II introduces the love interest between Leslie, the hostage, and Teresa, a young maid in the house who has, quite improbably, come from a convent school to work in the brothel. She had worked briefly for a family in Drumcondra, but, since her virtue was threatened by a clerical student, she left her employment. "As far as that's concerned," says Meg, "you'll be a lot safer here" (124). In many ways, of course, Teresa is safer in the brothel than she was with her clerical student; for the inmates of Behan's brothel are more honest and are kinder than people in the outside world.

That Teresa is one of the dominant voices of life in the play is made clear near the end of Act I when she criticizes Monsewer's ridiculous eulogy of the boy who is to die in Belfast jail. Says Monsewer: "It does not make me unhappy. It does not make me unhappy, but proud. It makes me proud and happy to know that the old cause is not dead yet, and that there are still young men willing to go out and die for Ireland. . . . He will, he will. With God's help, tomorrow morning he will be in the company of the heroes. It warms my heart to think of it" (124–25). Immediately after, Teresa talks to Meg:

TERESA: Wasn't that the ridiculous talk that old one had out of him about the boy being hung?

MEG: Well, Monsewer doesn't look at it like any ordinary person. Monsewer is very given to Ireland and to things of that sort.

TERESA: I think he's an old idiot.

MEG: An idiot? Monsewer was in all the biggest colleges of England, I'll have you know.

TERESA: It's all the same where he was. He is mad to say that the death of a young man made him happy.   (125)

Leslie also is on the side of life. When he is dragged into the brothel at the end of the first act, he breaks into song. In spite of

his rather dark prospects, he shouts out "There's No Place on
Earth Like the World."

Reminiscent of Romeo and Juliet's situation, the young people
in this play have in their background feuding countries rather
than families; and their religions place them poles apart as well—
Leslie is Protestant; Teresa, a Catholic. That this relationship
could survive at all is unlikely, but to emphasize man's overwhelming life force, Behan places the couple in one of the most
unlikely and sterile of all places—a brothel—and adds the additional complication of the young man's death sentence. Even the
continuity of the relationship is broken. Guards burst in; Monsewer enters playing bagpipes (Soldier: "The only good thing
about those pipes is they don't smell" [139]), and Teresa is forced
to hide under the bed.

Nevertheless, the two young people manage to share a great
deal of time, and they finally commune sexually as well as ver-
bally. Their conversation largely concerns their youth and their
innocence, even though, just before they hop into bed together,
they indulge in a bit of clowning which verges on the bawdy. A
good many prudish viewers and critics are, in fact, so shocked by
the sexual relationship between Teresa and Leslie that they ignore
the fact that it is the only natural act in the entire play. Every
other action is a perversion—of love, of patriotism, of life itself.

Critic Stephen Ryan considers the entire play a contest between
the world of sham and evil and that of innocence and love. However, maintains Ryan, "Behan loses his great chance when he
allows his young innocents to fall from grace; and what might
have been justified as a modern morality play breaks down completely." [10] Ryan's criticism, as well as others like it, seemingly ig-
nores the theme which Behan is trying to develop. The two young
people are concerned with life and the present. Everyone else in
the brothel is concerned with death and the past. In the midst of
unimaginable sterility—commercial sex, homosexuality, destructive chauvinism—the young people assert life. If Behan had indeed intended a "modern morality play," the moral he intended
seems aptly expressed by Meg: "What's wrong with a bit of comfort on a dark night?" (152).

The night is indeed dark, for Leslie learns in this act what all
the other inhabitants of the brothel have known for some time—
he is definitely to be shot. Yet, when his execution is confirmed,

Leslie does not ask for sympathy; he breaks into rollicking song. He simply refuses to recognize his mortality.

As in Act I, in Act II Behan supplements his demonstrations of man's indomitable vitality with an assertion of man's inescapable foolishness. Satire is present even in the Leslie-Teresa scenes:

> TERESA: Our best time was the procession we had for the Blessed Virgin on May Day—
> SOLDIER: Procession for who?
> TERESA: Shame on you, the Blessed Virgin. Anyone would think you were a Protestant.
> SOLDIER: I am, girl.
> TERESA: Oh, excuse me.
> SOLDIER: That's all right. Never think about it myself.   (147)

Certainly when two young people are speaking innocently and sincerely to each other the distinction between Protestant and Catholic is indeed irrelevant.

In Act II, Monsewer is still the most ridiculous of a houseful of ridiculous people. At one point in Act II, while reminiscing with young Leslie about England, Monsewer forgets for a moment that he has left all that behind.

> MONSEWER: You can't even speak the Queen's English . . . No background, no tradition, nothing.
> SOLDIER: Oh yes I have. They gave us all that at the Boys Home. Cricket, team spirit, fair play—we took all that.
> MONSEWER: Do you play cricket?
> SOLDIER: Yes, sir. Do you like a game?
>
> .   .   .   .
>
> MONSEWER: Ah, cricket, by jove that takes me back. Fetch the pianist, Patrick. Strange how this uncouth youth has brought back half-forgotten memories of summers long past.   (142)

The exchange ends with Monsewer's absurd rendition of "The Captains and the Kings," and it is clear that, either as lapsed Englishman or as stupidly sentimental Irishman, he is a mad fool; and Monsewer's madness is symbolic of the world he inhabits, a world which concerns itself more with death than with life.

V *Act III*

As the execution draws near in Act III, the tension mounts. And, as in *The Quare Fellow*, when the execution is approaching, all the characters are affected. Tempers are short. Pat mourns the "old days," maintaining that "these white-faced loons with their trench coats, berets, and teetotal badges have no right to call themselves members of the I.R.A." (159). Meg snaps back at him: "They've as much right to their drilling and marching, their revolvers and generals and sacrifices and white horses and wounds and last dying words and glory as you had" (160). Pat holds out for a little pity, however, by reminding Meg that "It was at Mullinger, on the field of battle that I lost my leg . . . What a battle! The fight went on for three days without cease. . . . The town was nothing but red fire and black smoke and the dead piled high on the roads" (158–59). But Meg reminds Pat that he had previously told a different story: "You told me there was only one man killed . . . and he was the County Surveyor out measuring the road and not interfering with politics one way or another" (159). The poor county surveyor is in the same position as Leslie —"not interfering with politics one way or another." Both are condemned by human stupidity.

Obviously, the tone of the satire is becoming more bitter. The emphasis has shifted from good-natured banter to the biting cry of the hostage that "an Englishman can die as well as an Irishman or anybody else in the world" (168). Behan's assertion of the absurd things man does to man in the name of causes and faiths makes it more difficult for one to laugh good-naturedly at the foolish but dangerous maniacs which inhabit his brothel. But, whenever Behan momentarily threatens to make a really vitriolic point about man's stupidities, he overwhelms it with the great vitality which his characters evince even in their impossible situation. Unlikely as it seems, they continue to romp, to sing, and to carry on in the manner which caused some reviewers to miss entirely the seriousness of the play, especially that of the third act.

Behan's own deep feelings, however, do show occasionally— in a casual statement by Leslie, "At least the poor bloke in Belfast has peace, and tomorrow he'll have nuns and priests and the whole works to see him on his way" (176)—and also in Teresa's presenting to Leslie the most meaningful gift she can think of—

her religious medal. These moments of sentiment and obvious sincerity are brief, however, for Behan is primarily concerned with pointing out the ridiculousness of actions dictated by a hollow faith; and he seems almost embarrassed—in the presence of his serious satire—to admit that anyone can believe in anything.

Act III and the play conclude in a wild melee in which young Leslie, the hostage, is killed; and the only natural, worthwhile relationship in the play is abruptly ended. Though there is a certain crudeness in the affair between Teresa and Leslie, there also exists a certain tenderness. Even though he suspects his death is near, Leslie can concern himself with Teresa: "I'd like all the blokes in the billet to see you. 'Cos they've all got pictures on the walls— well, I never had any pictures, but now I've got you. Then we'd go to Belfast and have a bloody good time together" (177). And Teresa, after Leslie's death, speaks some moving lines as she mourns Leslie at the same time she attacks Pat: "Ah, it was not Belfast Jail or the six counties that was bothering you—but your lost youth and your crippled leg. I will never forget him. He died in a strange land and at home he has no one. I will never forget you Leslie. Never, till the end of time" (182).

The fact that Leslie is killed accidentally in the exchange of shots between the police and the I.R.A. heightens the irony of *The Hostage* and more forcefully brings home Behan's satiric message. The Irish and the English, in fact all mankind, says Behan, enslave themselves with hollow, selfish systems which would stamp out life itself and everything that is beautiful in life. Whether man kills his fellow man out of sheer viciousness, foolish pride, or mere bumbling makes little difference. Man follows his penchant for paying attention to the nonessentials of his existence, and he causes untold suffering—all the more horrible because it is needless.

Pat, near the end of the play, attempts to comfort Teresa:

PAT: Don't cry, Teresa—and don't blame anybody for it. Nobody meant to kill him.
TERESA: But he's dead.   (182)

Leslie is most certainly dead; and, though Pat says no one is to blame, Teresa and Behan will not allow the guilty to escape so easily. All that a man should be—devoted to life and to the strengthening of communion between human beings—is demonstrated in the brief relationship between Teresa and Leslie. What man more often is is demonstrated in the foolish conflict between the Irish and the English. Again, the gap between what man should be and what he is provides Behan with the major vehicle for his satire.

The other aspect of Behan's comic genius is also present in the conclusion of *The Hostage;* for, though Leslie is dead, he arises and sings "The Bells of Hell." This song, of course, is Behan's tribute to the indomitable vitality of mankind. Man may be foolish enough to kill his fellow, but the spirit of man, as well as his love for life, somehow endures. The circumstances of man's environment, and his own weakness, would leave little hope that he can perhaps ever live the kind of life his imagination holds possible. That man does not acquiesce helplessly—that he shakes his fist at the universe—is to Behan sad, admirable, absurd, and funny.

CHAPTER 5

Borstal Boy

> I never saw a man who looked
> With such a wistful eye
> Upon that little tent of blue
> Which prisoners call the sky,
> And at every drifting cloud that went
> With sails of silver by.
> —*"The Ballad of Reading Gaol"*

BEHAN'S detractors are wonderfully stubborn. Just as they have said that Joan Littlewood wrote *The Quare Fellow* and *The Hostage*, they say some other mysterious angel did *Borstal Boy*. The truth is, of course, that Behan himself, with a good deal of bad editorial advice, wrote *Borstal Boy*, the first two-thirds of which is extremely moving and excellently written.

I *Early Versions of* Borstal Boy

Some of this book was obviously written while Behan was in prison; and the June, 1942, issue of *The Bell* included a short piece entitled "I Become a Borstal Boy" by nineteen-year-old Brendan Behan. In this short piece, Behan describes an incident in the prison chapel, a conversation which he had had with an accused murderer, and his own appearance in court which had brought him a sentence of three years Borstal detention. When these same incidents appeared in *Borstal Boy* sixteen years later, Behan expanded them considerably, adding some fine touches not present in the piece in *The Bell*. *The Bell* version, though rather interesting because of the uniqueness of its subject matter, has a reportorial tone and reads a bit like an exposé. The final version possesses much greater warmth, and the experiences which Behan describes are much more skillfully integrated with the view of life which he is attempting to assert. In any case, the significant differences between "I Become a Borstal Boy" and the final version of

Borstal Boy indicate that Behan was a conscious artist who not only reworked his materials, but attempted to improve them by revision.

Other obvious evidence of Behan's early interest in writing and his early mastery of the craft exists in the files of *Envoy* magazine, published from 1949 to 1951. These files contain two Behan typescripts,[1] though neither was published in *Envoy*, that are early versions of bits of *Borstal Boy*. One, called "Bridewell Revisited," which was published in *Points* in the winter issue of 1951–52, carries a note in Behan's hand: "A bit that I am not ashamed of, the title supplied by John Ryan for whom my affection is tenacious, invincible and reckless." "Bridewell Revisited" is an account of Behan's arrest and his early friendship with Charlie, the English sailor who plays a major role in *Borstal Boy*. The other segment, apparently never published, deals with the beating of a fellow Irishman, Callan, and the events shortly before Behan was transferred from Walton Prison to the Borstal institution.

Both pieces are infused with an insuppressible vitality, and neither possesses quite this vitality when it appears in revised form in *Borstal Boy*. The typescript of "Bridewell Revisited" contains a four-letter word in nearly every line, but the final effect of these words is by no means disgusting. They assert clearly and economically the brazenness and bravado of Behan's attitude toward the English. The four-letter words which the arresting officers use on Behan are also effective in that they serve to communicate the outrage which the officers experience and, strangely enough, the tenderness and respect they feel for the young Irish rebel.[2] The book version of *Borstal Boy* invariably cuts or disguises four-letter words, and, the typescript and the *Points* version is clearly superior; for the tone of immaturity, irresponsibility, and foolish adolescence is more clearly maintained. It fits both the truth of Behan's character and the thematic requirements of his book that the Brendan Behan whom the English arrested in Liverpool was immature and foolish, too much so to hold his tongue about anything.

In attempting to "clean" and "tighten" *Borstal Boy*, Behan's editors may have done him a disservice. Two passages which exist in the typescript and in the *Points* "Bridewell Revisited" but which do not exist in the book version of *Borstal Boy* indicate that Behan might have been badly advised. In *Points* and in the typescript,

after Behan is taken to the headquarters of the Liverpool C.I.D.
he is asked to make a statement:

> In accordance with instructions from the organisation, I refused to
> answer questions. I agreed to make a statement, with a view to propa-
> ganda, for the Republic. Ultimately I suppose, for myself. Revolution-
> ary politics are forms of acting. Ghandi ne'er cast a clout, nor Goering
> ne'er turned a jowl camerawards with more care than I took with that
> statement.
> "My name is Brendan Behan. I came over here to fight for the Irish
> Worker's and small Farmer's republic, for a full and free life for my
> fellow countrymen north and south, and for the removal of the baneful
> influence of British imperialism from Irish affairs. God save Ireland." [3]

In the book version, the references to Ghandi, Goering, and revolutionary politics are replaced by ones to speeches made by other
imprisoned Irishmen: "I often read speeches from the dock, and
thought the better of the brave and defiant men that made them
so far from friends or dear ones" (6).[4]

The substitution is unfortunate, for it hints at a maturity which
Behan in fact did not possess when he was arrested in Liverpool.
The reference to "acting" and the unlikely juxtaposition of Ghandi
and Goering better reflect the mood of fright and inexperience
which is the most appropriate one at this stage of the young Borstal boy's development. The second passage from "Bridewell Revisited" which was excised from the book version of *Borstal Boy*
concerns masturbation. In *Points* and the typescript the description is singularly effective:

> Oh, Cathlin ni Houlihan, your way is a thorny way. Much you knew
> about it, Yeats, yourself and Maud Gonne, bent over a turf fire reading
> Ronsard.
> A horny way, you mean. Wonder if Emmet did it in prison, or de
> Valera? Who'd have thought the old man had so much blood in him?
> And, tingling all over, pleasantly tired from the exercise, I fell
> asleep.[5]

The same passage was drained of its blood as it appeared in *Borstal Boy*:

> I put my mind on other things. It was at least and at last permissible
> to a man in my position.
> Then I settled myself more comfortably and wondered if anyone else

had done it in the same position. I didn't like to mention them by name, even in my mind. Some of them had left the cell for the rope or the firing squad. More pleasantly tired, from the exercise, I fell asleep.
(10)

Nearly every page of "Bridewell Revisited" is overflowing with vitality, love of life, meaningful naïveté. Nearly every page of the same segment as it appears in *Borstal Boy* seems somehow short of the mark, indefinite, and suppressed. A complete text of *Borstal Boy* as Behan wrote it does not exist, for he apparently destroyed it. Therefore it is impossible to assert definitely that the last three hundred and fifty pages of *Borstal Boy* as printed are terribly inferior to those same pages as Behan wrote them. Behan's first twenty pages, however, are so far superior to those finally appearing in *Borstal Boy* that one can reasonably wonder whether the book might have been a better work had Behan had a less conservative editor.

II *The Publication Party and Reviews*

With much fanfare *Borstal Boy* was published in October, 1958; and the Hutchison party given in honor of the author was a great success, as Michael Campbell's account in the *Irish Times* suggests:

At the center of the room stood the more human reality, large, flushed and tousled, with an old coat spread wide to reveal scarlet braces, and an unequivocal voice that warmly welcomed arriving guests and invited them to find a blankin' drink.

The worst-dressed person in the room was on this occasion the most important. Mr. Brendan Behan has hit London rather like Mr. Somerset Maugham, in his youth; it is surely beyond all imagination to think of two people more dissimilar hitting anywhere. Mr. Behan's new play "The Hostage" has left the London theatre critics breathless and invigorated. His first play "The Quare Fellow," a former success, is shortly to be televised. (This winter it will be running in Paris and New York, and the film rights are sold.)

His "Borstal Boy," officially published this week, was preceded by continual fanfares and has already received critical acclaim.[6]

When the party threatened to become dull, Patrick Campbell offered to sing "The Old Musheroon." When the revelers politely rejected Campbell, his song did not materialize. Behan, though, was equal to the occasion, and boldly sang "Oh the Praties Over There They Were Small." [7] Various other authors were present, but it was left to Mrs. Valentin Iremonger, wife of the distinguished Irish poet and statesman, to favor the company with the next song, one in Irish. Immediately Behan and Hugh Delargey, M.P., gave a lusty rendering of "The Bold Fenian Men," and soon the party erupted into a series of anti-British songs. As Michael Campbell reports, "In short, hilarity was general." The Hutchison representatives had obviously not counted on such a successful party, but with their nervous British smiles they carried it off.

The same page of the *Irish Times* which details the publishers' party also includes a hackneyed Hutchison advertisement—three tousled heads of Behan, each separated from its fellow by a journalistic ejaculation: "'A bomb of a book,' Kenneth Alsop, *Daily Mail;* 'Excellent . . . vivid,' Maurice Richardson, *The Observer;* 'A natural writer,' Cyril Connolly, *Sunday Times.*" Also on this page *Borstal Boy* is reviewed by Martin Sheridan, who was able to perceive no structure at all in the book and who adds dashes to those already supplied by the publishers. "F——s" becomes a proper "——s"; "be God" becomes "be——." "The blanks," says Sheridan, "are mine. Mr. Behan used ball ammunition." [8] The blanks, indeed, in a quite different sense are Mr. Sheridan's. Behan did not use "ball ammunition"; he used the language really used by men in a state of oppression.

Few reviews of *Borstal Boy* have done it justice. In general, the reviews range from those which are products of advance publicity releases and a few pages of skimming on the part of the reviewer to those which make the profane language of *Borstal Boy* their major point of departure. Of the former sort of review, Sheridan's in the *Irish Times* is a good example; of the latter, Orville Prescott's *New York Times* review serves. In Prescott's opinion, it was "bad editing and bad writing to allow so much profanity." [9] Only a few reviews, of which John Wain's is a fine example, perceived the art and the truth of *Borstal Boy:* "We are left with the impression of having read two distinct books, one grim and terrifying, the other light and farcical. But there is no perceptible join; one shades into the other. . . . Mr. Behan is no gifted leprechaun. He is a highly conscious, craftsmanlike, accomplished writer—a type never more needed than today." [10]

III Borstal Boy *as a Novel of Adolescence*

Behan frequently referred to *Borstal Boy* as a novel, and it is probably more fruitful to read it as such, rather than as an autobiography; for the story which Behan tells ranges beyond the individual story of the boy Brendan Behan to become a story of the adolescent idealist facing the real world—innocence confronting experience. As such, it has much in common with novels such as Herman Melville's *Redburn*, Mark Twain's *Huckleberry Finn*, and J. D. Salinger's *The Catcher in the Rye*. In these three novels, as in *Borstal Boy*, the adolescent hero, carrying with him his innocence and idealism, confronts a world which is cynical, cruel, and completely out of harmony with what it should be. This is the material of satire in these American classics and also in Behan's book. In all, though the adolescent is continually shocked by his contact with the cynicism of the adult world (says Melville, very early in *Redburn*, "there is no misanthrope like a boy disappointed"), he still laughs and causes his audience to laugh; through this laughter he asserts that he is alive, and not only accepts the burden of existence, but enjoys it as well. Only *Huckleberry Finn* and *Borstal Boy*, however, have a hero who is rather uncomplaining. Both Huck and the young Brendan Behan tend to observe without bitterness or self-pity.

Unfortunately, another resemblance exists between *Huckleberry Finn* and *Borstal Boy*. The concluding sections of both books are seriously flawed. In the last sections of his book, Twain violated theme and character as he had constructed them earlier in the book. Behan cannot be accused in such dignified terms, for he seems in the last hundred pages or so of *Borstal Boy* to have been stimulated mainly by his publishers' requirement for a set number of words. The last hundred pages of *Borstal Boy* nearly destroy the fine work that Behan did in the first two hundred and sixty. Yet the first two hundred and sixty pages of *Borstal Boy* are excellent; and here, as in his other major works, the two major aspects of Behan's comic genius shine forth: he is marvelously satiric, and he is marvelously alive.

The book opens with Behan's arrest in a Liverpool rooming

house. The moment the police have handcuffed him, they begin
their questioning; and the chief arresting officer challenges Behan
to name the six counties the I.R.A. wants to liberate from the English:

> "You're a silly lot of chaps, going on with this lot. You don't even
> know why you're bloody well doing it. It's supposed to be about Parti-
> tion. About the Six Counties. Well, I've interviewed a lot of your fel-
> lows, and God blind old Reilly if one of them could even name the
> bloody things. Not all six, they couldn't. Go on, now, you. The whole
> six, mind."
> I began. "Antrim, Armagh."
> The sergeant counted on his fingers. "Right, that's two you've got."
> "Down, Derry, and Fermanagh and . . ."
> "Right, five you got. Come on, the last one."
> "Down, Derry, and Fermanagh . . . and . . ."
> "There you are, Paddy, what did I tell you?" He shook his head
> triumphantly.
> I left out County Tyrone, for he was a nice old fellow.   (5)

This scene is remarkably similar to the one early in *The Catcher in
the Rye* in which Holden Caulfield has a last interview with his
history teacher, Mr. Spencer. Spencer lectures Holden on his poor
performance on the examination; but, contrary to what would
normally be expected in such a situation, the child comforts the
adult. Holden says, "Well, you could see he felt pretty lousy
about flunking me. So I shot the bull for a while. I told him I was
a real moron, and all that stuff. I told him how I would've done
exactly the same thing if I'd been in his place, and how most people don't appreciate how tough it is being a teacher. That kind of
stuff. The old bull." [11]

In the scene from *Borstal Boy* and that from *The Catcher in the
Rye*, the tone is mildly satiric. In both, the adolescent is consider-
ate and honest, and the adult seems too much in the power of the
mechanical requirements of his job to be either kind or truthful.
Yet both boys remain aware of what the right and human action
is; and, in spite of the fact that the adult world would turn them
into unthinking machines, they remain human and alive.

IV   *Behan and Charlie*

On his first day in prison, Behan meets Charlie, the young sailor
who is to be his friend or "china" throughout imprisonment. The

innocence and kindness of these two boys, both of whom have
sinned against the Crown, are sensitively and economically described. A short conversation in the jail rest room between Charlie
and the young Behan is illustrative:

"I only came in last night," said I, rubbing my chin, "I'm not so bad."
I had shaved four times in my life.
"You Irish?"
I nodded.
"Well, there's a lot of blokes round our way are Irish. Went to R.C.
school and all, they did. We all used to sing Irish songs. Confidentially,"
he lowered his voice, "I don't like these Lancashire blokes, myself.
Bloody lot of swede-bashers. I'm from Croydon. Know where that is,
Paddy?"
"Of course I do. It's in London, where the airport is."
"That's it. Smashing place it is and all, Croydon. Not like this hole.
I was picked up here for some screwing jobs. Here and in Manchester—
another bloody graveyard. But some good screwing jobs to be done
round there. What are you in for, Pad? Boozer battle or something?"
"No, I'm in over the I.R.A. Explosives."
"Are you———!"
"I am, though."
"Straight up?"
"Straight up."
"Cor, you won't half cop it for that lot." There was no hostility in
his voice but almost concern. "Fix that vest, will you, Pad? Just shove
it down a bit."
He turned round, and I shoved down an inch of his vest that was
showing above his blouse. "There is a bit of soap behind your ear."
He handed me a towel and I wiped, carefully, the back of his ears.
"Thanks, Paddy."   (12)

One boy is Irish, the other English; but neither has yet become
imprisoned by his nationality. Each relates to the other naturally
and humanely. The counterpoint to this natural and humane action, however, is constantly in the background. The prison, its
steel bars, its warders, and its mechanistic requirements continually intrude. As the young prisoners are led to their cells, they bid
each other good-by:

"Bye, Pad," whispered Charlie. He tipped me with his elbow, and
went into his cell.

"I'll put a double lock on you," said the screw. "You London blokes are so leery. Regular bloody lot of 'Oudinis, down there."

I was left on my own.

"Now, Guy Fawkes, lead on to the dungeons."

I went down the stairs.

"Plenty of accommodations 'ere. You've got an 'ole suite of rooms to yourself."

I said nothing.

"And I bet you ain't satisfied. That's the Irish, all over. Never done cribbing."

He opened the door. "And fold up them bloody blankets. You ain't sleeping with the pigs now, you know."   (14)

So the prison has the final say, but it is clear that no prison, no system, can break these boys. They refuse to become ciphers. They assert their humanity continually—sometimes through laughter, sometimes through kindness. All men should act as humanely as these boys; most men do not; thus, in *Borstal Boy* that lapse from the ideal which is an essential part of satire.

V *Lyricism, Romanticism, and Vitality*

The organization of *Borstal Boy* is loose and imperfect; yet, taken in bits and pieces, it is moving and wonderfully lyric. For instance, the second chapter of *Borstal Boy*, which deals largely with the transfer of Behan from the Dale Street lockup to the Walton Prison, contains some superb descriptive passages: "The bells of a hundred churches crashed and banged on my ears all morning. It was not so bad then, because I like the morning time, and the day did not begin to get gloomy till the light faded from the sky in the afternoon. Then the bells began again, and in defenceless misery I bore them" (22). And his despair is touching:

I could not even walk, but sat huddled on the bed in my blankets, with tears in my mind and in my heart, and wishing I could wake up and find out that I had only been dreaming this, and could wake up at home, and say, well, that's how it would be if you were pinched in England, and not attend any more parades, and drop out of the I.R.A. and attend more to my trade, and go out dancing or something, and get married; and if, watching an Easter parade and listening to the crash of drums and scream of the pipes as the four battalions of the Dublin Brigade went into the slow march and gave "eyes left," as they passed the G.P.O. with their banners lowered, and the crowds either side of O'Connell Street baring their heads, I felt my blood go to my scalp—then I could always remind myself of the time I dreamt I was captured in Liverpool, and bring my blood back to my feet.   (22)

In this chapter, too, Behan's essential Romanticism is evident. Just before the warders give him an especially brutal beating, Behan compares himself to the Irish folk hero Cuchulainn: "Young Cuchulainn, after the battle of the ford of Ferdia, on guard the gap of Ulster, with his enemies ringed round him, held his back to a tree and, supported by it, called on the gods of death and grandeur to hold him up till his last blood flowed" (34). During the beating, Behan is realistic enough to cover his crotch; but the warders cannot beat out of him either his essential humanity or his innocent, idealistic way of looking at the world. Even God is called to account for not putting things together in a more sensible way. When Behan observes the fat, ugly body of an old prisoner, Donohoe, he protests that the young prisoners should become old, fat, and sick:

Jesus, it must be the terrible thing to get fat, I thought. Porter it was that fattened people in my own family, and it would be a hard thing not to drink porter with every other decent man, and maybe stand filling your pipe with your back to the counter, and maybe talk of the time you were in jail in England, still that day was a good bit from us yet. . . . Donohoe stood with some other men prisoners, and their bent old legs and twisted buniony toes on a line, the way, I thought, looking from the smooth neatness of Charlie and Ginger and me, that God would have a lot to do forgiving Himself for sentencing us all that would live long enough, to get like that.   (41)

The ugliness, the injustice of the world Behan could not abide; but, before his first stretch in prison was over, he was to experience a good deal more injustice and stupidity, more of the basic absurdity of human existence.

In the third chapter of *Borstal Boy* the strange systems which man constructs against himself become terribly clear, but it is just as clear that no system can stifle the life spirit of young Brendan Behan. The chapter, very short, consists of a naïve yet satiric description of the morning "slop out" and inspection. Each night the prisoner is locked in his cell with his chamber pot, and the cell is not opened until the next morning, at which time, just before breakfast, the cell is unlocked and the chamber pots "slopped out" into a bucket carried round by an orderly—a lucky man, Behan remarks, for he is the same man who later carries breakfast to the prisoners and is able to steal a bit of food from the plates. After breakfast comes cell inspection, with the cleaned chamber pots and all the rest of the prisoner's kit laid out. To meet inspection, says Behan, "there was a shine on the cell furniture and the black glistening newly soaped floor and heavy smell of human excrement over the place that would make you respect the stern fishy eye and the stiff thin lip and the steady and high-purposed gaze of Englishmen doing their duty" (47).

According to prison regulations, it was a serious violation for any prisoner to use his chamber pot before inspection; sometimes, however, a prisoner could not deny nature. In one case the prisoner was "a Channel Islander, from a place called Peter's Port, and the screw said he'd bloody soon cure him of his dirty French habits" (48). Again Behan has observed, this time lewdly, that man defecates, man lives, in spite of prison or systems.

VI *The Consolation of the Church*

One system, however, which Behan hoped to gain sustenance from in prison was the Catholic Church; but it failed him. He had had difficulty before with the life-destroying bent of Catholicism, though when he was young and found life rather simple he found himself more in harmony with the Church: "I had been extra religious when a kid, and the day I made my First Communion I had prayed to God to take me, as Napoleon prayed, when I would go straight to Heaven. I was a weekly communicant for years after, and in spasms, especially during Lent, a daily one. Then I had difficulties, when I was thirteen or so, with myself and sex" (53). Communion and the whole ritual of the church would have been an important comfort to Behan in prison, yet when he was excommunicated he was denied this comfort.

The Church did have its consolations, not, however, the abstract dry and wilted spiritual ones which usually gladden the hearts of the clergy. The comfort the Church offered the prisoners was much more concrete—a break in the routine, a chance for a bit of exercise, a chance to talk to fellow prisoners, and occasionally a good sermon about the really important things in life. In the latter category is the sermon which Behan heard on his first Christmas

Day in prison. The priest begins by assuring the prisoners that "Christmas was a time of prayer as well as a time for enjoying yourself" (106). The enjoyment, however, seems to be more important to the priest than the prayer. Certainly this is the attitude of the prisoners, and they very much appreciate the priest's lapse:

"We make rejoicing, and think with love all the time even as we break the crackling of the goose, even as we savour the tender white meat of the turkey."

The chokey merchants in the front seats never took their eyes off the priest, and he looked kindly back at us all, and went on with the sermon.

"As we pour the sauce over that homely symbol of our own dear Christian land, the plum pudding, heavy, dark, rich and laden rarely with fruits of sunnier climes, Spain usually, and Italy, and while we enjoy the wine, as Christians should for, as I think it was Belloc remarked, it was given us in the first miracle, and liqueurs are to this day made by Carthusians, Dominicans, Benedictines, and if I may mention, in this our own dear land, at Buckfast, the monks make a good wine, but," here he smiled and we smiled with him, "in accordance with what I suppose is the traditionally more austere tradition of this, called by William Shakespeare, whom, as you know, lived and died in the Old Faith, 'sceptered isle' for medicinal purposes only. Or as we pour ourselves a foaming glass of ale, and draw on our cigar——"

The prisoners drew their breath in unison with the preacher, and some of the fellows on punishment swallowed and rubbed their mouths with the backs of their hands.   (107)

Better than Christmas was Easter, which Behan celebrated with his fellow prisoners in the Feltham allocation center. Again the appeal of the Church is emphasized in terms other than those one would normally expect. Quite simply the only reason that Behan and his fellow prisoners attend services is to escape the restriction of the cell and the work party. For this reason, in fact, two of Behan's friends are temporarily converted to Catholicism. Charlie, a Church of England boy, and "Chewlips," who has been to church only once in his life, find the appeal of the Catholic Church especially strong during Holy Week. The Roman Catholics were allowed a service every day from Palm Sunday until Easter Sunday. The "C of E" and the other denominations were to have only the usual Easter Sunday service. Charlie and Chewlips are quickly converted, for the novelty of an hour in any church is more enjoyable than an hour sewing mailbags, the usual work detail.

After initial instructions by Behan on making the sign of the cross and other details of ritual, Charlie and Chewlips go to the church service with the "R.C.'s" and become deeply involved in the religious experience. Chewlips and Charlie, lately converted, seem in fact to observe the service in more detail than do some of those prisoners who were born into the faith, though Joe, a friend of Behan's and a Catholic as well, gets into the spirit of things very well. Joe, in jail for rape, proves that he does not necessarily play favorites. The priest conducting the service is "followed by two altar boys, wearing soutanes and lace surplices over their Borstal shirts and shorts. Joe made a remark about the smaller one, a boy of about seventeen with dark hair, ruddy cheeks and great reverence. When they bowed going up towards the altar, Joe pretended to put his hand up this altar boy's surplice" (171).

Behan reports that he laughed at Joe's filthy gesture, but he feels obligated to tell why: "I would have been very angry and violently angry about such behaviour in a Catholic church before my time in Walton, but why should I be angry, and stick up for them, who wouldn't stick up for me, but hounded and insulted me worse than the British Protestants?" (171–72). The truth comes at the end of Behan's comment, "What the hell did I care about them or their services, except to pass an hour and enjoy it, like anyone else" (172).

It remains for Chewlips to catch the real inspiration of the services:

On Spy Wednesday, Chewlips and Charlie were so confident that they fell in before Joe and myself and down we went to the chapel. The little Italian priest gave us a long and sorrowful account of the agony in the garden and of our Lord's betrayal by Judas.

Chewlips followed this with breathless attention, and muttered some comments about Judas.

"——ing grass-'opper, ——ing bastard, just like me."

"And Jesus said to him, Judas, dost thou betray the Son of Man with a kiss?"

"Just like me," whispered Chewlips, "——ing bastard, we're going round in to Russell Street—"

"Kip in," said Charlie, in a fierce whisper, "you'll get us done."

"And," went on the priest, "they that were about Him, seeing what would follow, said to him, Lord, shall we strike with the sword?"

"That's it," said Chewlips, "carve the bastard up."   (174)

In all of these episodes in which the church is concerned, the innocent animal vitality of Behan and his companions has clearly risen above the dry, soul-destroying abstractions of the church and the prison. The boys, Behan the first among them, simply cannot accept systems which seem to have so little relevance to basic human realities. As Behan says much later in *Borstal Boy,* when noting that the comic view seems to be the proper one since man has so little time he should not waste it on heroic and religious foolishness, "such is the condition of man in this old world and we better learn to put up with it, such as it is, for I never saw much hurry on parish priests in getting to the next one, nor on parsons or rabbis, for the matter of that; and as they are all supposed to be the experts on the next world, we can take it that they have heard something very unpleasant about it which makes them prefer to stick it out in this one for as long as they can" (257).

VII *Enlargement of Sympathies*

Another abstraction which Behan rises above in *Borstal Boy* is his hatred of the English. At the end of his Borstal confinement Behan would not have sworn allegiance to the English crown, but he had learned that the quarrels of nations are largely irrelevant to the relationship between individuals. Two of Behan's closest friends in prison are English boys, and for these friends his loyalty is limitless. In the name of friendship, Charlie and Ginger jovially insult Behan's religion and his country. Behan is simply too alive and too honest to allow these two oppressive abstractions to take precedence over friendship. Behan's training still influences him, however; his loyalties are not lightly held for he thinks himself disloyal in preferring his friends to the cause of the I.R.A.: "I'd sooner be with Charlie and Ginger and Browny in Borstal than with my own comrades and countrymen any place else. It seemed a bit disloyal to me, that I should prefer to be with boys from English cities than with my own countrymen and comrades from Ireland's hills and glens" (118).

Behan is always aware of the failures of the English: "Towards the end of January, there was an appeal by the two Irishmen that had been sentenced to death at Birmingham before Christmas. I knew the man that had planted the bomb and it was neither of the men that had been sentenced. But that would not matter very much to the English. . . . Only England would shove on all this old insulting hypocrisy and tell you in the next breath that they were desperately careful that every foreigner the world over should know that justice had been done according to the law" (113). But Behan is also aware that "Everyone has their own way of looking at things and you couldn't blame them for taking a favourable view of their own kicking once they were kicking you in their own country and not they being kicked by someone else in someone elses'" (83). The English, Behan realizes, are human beings, no better, certainly no worse, than Irishmen, Americans, or Chinese. It is simply the human being that is morally limited.

VIII   *The Accommodation and the Pain*

Behan accommodated himself well to prison life. Some sections of *Borstal Boy* seem almost idyllic. On the trip to Hollesley Bay "some fellow had got streamers, from where I do not know, and we had them flying out of the window, as if it was an excursion we were on. The P.O. went to the parcels containing our property and distributed our cigarettes. After a while they started singing" (193). Behan does not much like the gardening details he is assigned to at Hollesley Bay, but he enjoys being alive and out in the sun. "On a turn of a sod, my fork uncovered a golden apple as hard and as fresh as the day it fell there. I held it up and showed it to Mr. Sullivan in the next row and he smiled with his narrowed eyes and told me to go ahead and eat it. I took a few hurried bites from it and, with the juice sharp on my tongue, put it back in my pocket, and got on with the work, with the morning well advanced and the springtime steaming off the trees and grass" (223).

The pain of prison life is everpresent, however, and Behan is as aware of it as he is of the limited pleasures of his existence. Without sentimentality and with an eye sensitive to the evil which man does his fellows in the name of justice, Behan describes the terror of prison life:

A clean shirt was the beating they sometimes gave a prisoner beginning his punishment. They told him to strip and then when he had his
clothes half-off they would accuse him of resisting the search, beat
him, baton him on the kidneys, and on the thighs.

Our P.O. was the most feared. Now that he was no longer young and
active enough to lead the fray, he waited till the prisoner was stripped
naked by the other screws. Then he would catch him by the ballocks
and twist and pull on them. Putting his weight and swinging down out
of them, not abusing the prisoner or angry but rather the reverse, grunting and saying softly, "All right, all right, now, it will be over in a
minute." Grunting and perspiring with the effort. "There, there, it will
soon be over."

It usually was—the bloke passing out. They never hit a prisoner on
the face, but on the rest of him which would only be seen by the prison
doctor. Extras such as our P.O's performance were reserved for people
with a good long bit of time to do. Even if the prisoner was ruptured,
nobody would know, except prison officials, warders, prison doctors,
and clergymen.   (100)

And Behan often heightens his description of the sickness and
horror of prison life with an artful juxtaposition. One of the best
of these is his description of the beating of a fellow Irishman,
Callan. This account is sandwiched between segments of Ellen
Gaskell's *Cranford*, which Behan is reading in his cell at the time
Callan is being beaten. The black cruelty of Callan's suffering is
heightened by the contrast with the elegant and genteel supper
which Miss Barker is offering her guests. Miss Barker's friends
wonder whether or not to have a bit of cherry brandy. Behan
wonders how much damage the guards are doing to Callan, and
whether Brendan Behan is to be the next to be beaten.

Behan uses the same sort of device in describing the sexual
loneliness of prison life. In this case Hardy's *The Greenwood Tree*
is the genteel background against which Behan projects the harsh
reality of his existence:

I took my book and started celebrating with a bit of a read extra.
. . . Bejasus and no one could say that Dick Dewy wasn't getting every
chance of a running leap at Fancy Day. He brings over her furniture
up to the new house where she's to set up as the village schoolteacher;
and there he was sitting on his hunkers trying to get the fire going till
she'd make the first cup of tea in the house. . . . And a bed and all

in the house.—I heard tell the bed was a gift, far and wide in front of the standy-up job. . . . Ah, but Dick wasn't as green as he was cabbage-looking. "Dick, Dick, kiss me and let go instantly—here's somebody coming!"—it's me, Brendan Behan, 3501 H. M. Prison, Liverpool, Vol. Brendan Behan, 2nd Battalion, Dublin Brigade, Irish Republican Army. But I didn't, only started thinking about my cocoa and cheese tonight, maybe the last meal I'd eat for a while, and a man needed all his strength in the times that were in it. Not to be thinking of things like *that*.   (80)

Through it all, however, Behan is never bitter or insensitive. He protects the dull-witted Chewlips from the abuse of the other young prisoners. For Ken, the friendless rich kid, Behan's sympathy is boundless: "He was dead lonely, more lonely than I and with more reason. The other fellows might give me a rub about Ireland or about the bombing campaign, and that was seldom enough and I was never short of an answer, historically informed and obscene, for them. But I was nearer to them than they would ever let Ken be" (227). For himself, Behan says "I'd probably got away with more than I was ever punished for" (363). Truly, the Brendan Behan described in *Borstal Boy* is a kind, gentle, forgiving person.

In the last hundred pages of *Borstal Boy* Behan seems to be searching desperately for some experience worth communicating. He informs us, for instance, that his sister can sing "God Save the King" in backslang, that painters who work with fast-drying paint must work fast, that it would be great to be free again. With the exception of the last segment of the book, however, *Borstal Boy* is, as has been noted earlier, an excellent book, well written, sensitive, and wonderfully alive. In *Borstal Boy*, Behan has given us the story of a boy who refuses to let the world destroy his honesty and his vitality; and English literature is richer for Behan's having told his own story.

CHAPTER 6

Minor Works

Ireland is like that—a land of contrasts like every other country—rigid in some matters, free and easy in others. You can take it or leave it, and thats the end of my story and all I am going to tell you and thanks for coming along.

—*Brendan Behan's Island*

BRENDAN Behan's reputation will rest on those stories he told best—*The Quare Fellow, The Hostage, Borstal Boy*. He told many others, and many of them are very good—not particularly inspired, but neat and workmanlike as though intended to provide evidence for the argument that Behan was a writer with natural talent and industry, not a mere chancer.

I *The Scarperer*

In 1953, under the pseudonym of Emmet Street, Behan wrote *The Scarperer*, a tale of the Dublin and Paris underworld, which ran serially in the *Irish Times* in October and November of 1953. In 1964, the year of Behan's death, *The Scarperer* was published in book form and has since been translated into German by Annemarie and Heinrich Böll. Behan told Rae Jeffs that he wrote the story under a pseudonym because before 1953 he had written "pieces of pornography" for French magazines,[1] pieces which had not met with the approval of the "Dublin intelligentsia." Behan's employment of the pseudonym, however, seems yet another indication of his deeply felt insecurity. It is clear that the "Dublin intelligentsia" paid little attention to Behan even as late as the 1954 Dublin production of *The Quare Fellow*. Certainly in 1953 Behan was not known at all as a writer, and his overestimation of the attention which *The Scarperer* would receive was clearly a disguise designed to hide the fact that he was too unsure of his talents to put his own name on his story.

119

The reviews of the book version of *The Scarperer* were generally very perceptive. Emile Capouya in *The Saturday Review of Literature* accurately categorized the book as "the merest by-blow of Behan's genius," and noted that the book exhibits Behan's "gift for talk, but none of his gift for the talk that is the breath of life, that is, literature." [2] The *Times Literary Supplement* emphasized the honest craftsmanship which *The Scarperer* displays: "*The Irish Times* got value for its money; this is a professional job and good of its kind." [3] To Anne O'Neill Barna of the *New York Times Book Review*, *The Scarperer* is a suitable last testament: "It is a talkative story, a compendium of Dublin speech such as we are not likely to get again." [4] One of the most enthusiastic reviews asserted that "*The Scarperer* should invite favorable comparisons with the best work of Henry Green and John Hawkes." [5]

Although *The Scarperer* is not great literature, it does indicate that Behan could construct a plot, a smooth economical one in the best nineteenth-century tradition. The story opens at the Mendicity where the inhabitants of Dublin's skid row are discussing the results of the lottery that is run by a gentleman named Pig's Eye O'Donnell. Some say that Dunlavin has won, but others insist that Tralee Trembles, alias James Guiney, is the winner. At the Hot Wall, the side wall of a bakery kept warm by the ovens behind it, the truth is out. Dunlavin has won: "Tralee Trembles was only minding the ticket for him, because Dunlavin was lobby-watching this weather. He was barred in most of the lodging houses, and the ones he was let into were all full, so he slept on the landings of tenement houses and spent the price of his flop, when he had it, on chat. He had lately lost a pair of boots, given him at the mission, and Tralee Trembles took the ticket on account of him having a flop nearly always" (3). [6]

When Pig's Eye pays the winning ticket, worth two pounds, ten shillings, in the Shaky Man's, Dunlavin buys drinks all round; but, before the "glasses of chat" are properly consumed, a mysterious stranger enters the Shaky Man's and most incongruously orders a glass of lemonade. The stranger is a recently escaped convict named Eddie Collins whose mission is to get Tralee Trembles drunk and sent to Mountjoy prison where it is planned that he will serve unaware as a decoy to aid two other prisoners to escape. Collins' task is easy. Tralee Trembles gets fearfully drunk, throws a bottle through the window of the Shaky Man's, and is arrested and sent to Mountjoy. He is chloroformed by the hospital orderly, a trustee named Jerry Synnott, and placed in the bed of the Limey, alias James Kirke, alias Eric James Watt.

While Tralee lies unconscious in the Limey's bed, satisfying the guards that the Limey is still in his cell, Jerry and the Limey escape. The Limey is grateful, and is eager to pay the Scarperer, whose organization has carried out the escape, but the Scarperer and his men, Jerry and Lugs, keep the Limey with them in their hideout under the pretext of protecting him from the police. Actually the Scarperer has other plans for the Limey, who bears a close physical resemblance to a notorious French criminal called Pierre le Fou, and the "mad one" would find it very convenient if the police thought him dead. Le Fou has promised the Scarperer much more money than the organization can hope to make from the Limey's payment for his escape, so the Scarperer plans to drown the Limey and cause his body to be washed ashore on the French coast where it will hopefully be mistaken for Pierre le Fou.

The Scarperer's plan works well for a time. The Limey suspects nothing until the very instant his drugged body is thrown over the side of the Scarperer's ship into the sea: "He felt them lifting him and looked in a dazed and terrified appeal at the Scarperer and struggled to scream. 'I-I-I-aaaah.' 'Now,' said the Scarperer, and they heaved him over the rail and into the water and his cry was choked by the sea, and the trawler went on towards the French coast" (119). But, just as the Scarper and his henchmen, Eddie Collins, Jerry Synnott, and Lugs are enjoying the warm glow which comes from executing successfully a complicated plan, they are confronted in the streets of Paris by an elderly Irishwoman:

The elderly woman ran in front of them and shook her hands in their faces and in a Monkstown accent, that sounded like South Kerry on the alien air, screamed with fury:

"Murderers! I followed you from Dieppe, though it cost me dear in the car. Murderers! Murderers!" (124)

Lugs smashes the old lady in the face, but she struggles to her feet and "muttered through her bleeding lips: 'Murderers, murderers of our dumb brother.'" But the Irishwoman, Aunt Jeannie, has made a mistake. The Scarperer and his crew are not her men at

all. Aunt Jeannie is on foreign assignment for the Irish section of
the International Society for the Defence of the Horse, and she
mistakenly accuses the Scarperer and his men of importing horses
to France for slaughter; however, the Scarperer's organization has
merely killed a human being. Aunt Jeannie says later, after her
complaint to the police has resulted in a shootout in the Café
Bouillon, "They were the wrong men. I was shouting at them and
blaming them for something of which they were innocent" (149).

In the confrontation at the Bouillon, Pierre le Fou, who thinks
he has been betrayed by the Scarperer, avenges himself by shooting him; Pierre is in turn killed by the police. The survivors, Lugs,
Eddie Collins, and Jerry Synnott are jailed, ironically enough, not
for killing horses or Englishmen, but for "murdering one James
Guiney, by administering to him, or causing to be administered to
him, a noxious substance, to wit chloroform" (152). An added
ironical note is the charge of counterfeiting which the survivors of
the Scarperer's crew will have to face if they beat the murder
charge. It seems that Pierre le Fou had paid the Scarperer and his
men with fifty-three million thousand francs of counterfeit money.
As Jerry says, Pierre le Fou was nothing but a dirty crook.

The plot of *The Scarperer* is complicated enough to satisfy even
the most jaded of detective-story readers. Perhaps the greatest
tribute to Behan's imagination which *The Scarperer* contains,
however, is the wonderful gallery of underworld characters. Tralee Trembles, Dunlavin, and Pig's Eye are citizens of studied and
conservative habits compared to The Goofy One, Glimmers Gleason, Nancy Hand, Mrs. Genockey, Kilbeggen Kate, and Billy Boy.
Glimmers Gleason's place of business is on a Liffey bridge where,
wearing black spectacles and a "Blind from Birth" sign, he looks
for gullible souls who will put a few coins in his cup. Mrs. Genockey is a talented tavern singer, "famous along the Quay, on the
left-hand side as you go down" (8).

These denizens of the Dublin underworld are outdone, however, by the grotesques of Behan's Paris slums. Among these are
the Veritable Sage, who before being committed to an asylum in
his native United States ran an "Akademia of Dance and Song
and Mime and Greek Living. He wore a long white beard and
skirts of flannel, a leather belt, and sandals. His female disciples,
half a dozen fat old ladies who came to Paris at the same time as
himself, were similarly got up, except for the beard" (96). The

Bonapartist, who dresses in a long black coat and cocked hat, believes that, if one traveled to London, he would find "Billy Pitt still spinning his webs of intrigue from Ten Downing Street" (97). Le Mandarin was another old gentleman "of uncertain nationality, but with an extensive knowledge of a branch of English Literature consisting of treaties between H.M. Government and the late Imperial Government of China. He carried copies of these documents, English text one side and Chinese the other, and was always willing to read the Chinese bit, if the English person wanted to follow it on the other page. Most of them didn't but le Mandarin, amongst his accomplishments, had a knowledge of jujitsu and insisted on giving value for his entertainment" (97). Even stranger is M'sieu le Tramtrack, who was injured by a tram in the Boulevard Saint-Michel before World War I. M'sieu le Tramtrack's lawyer advised him to stay in bed until damages were awarded him, so for thirty years Tramtrack remained in bed, and was awarded full damages of seventy thousand francs in 1946. Strange as these characters are, however, Behan makes them seem almost normal. Even at their most grotesque, they are believable and obviously quite at home in the mad, capricious world which Behan constructs in *The Scarperer*.

The comedy in *The Scarperer* is marvelously done. The tavern scenes are full of the cynical hilarity which Behan could create so well. The laughter in *The Scarperer* is a bit different, however, from that which echoes throughout *The Quare Fellow, The Hostage,* and *Borstal Boy*. The satiric, corrective dimension seems almost totally absent in this book. The inhabitants of Behan's slums are simply too tired and too tolerant to deal even ephemerally with the ideal of man as he should be. They have been beaten down too much by the world. The assertive element, though, is much in evidence in the laughter of *The Scarperer*. Behan's slum dwellers have been beaten, but they have not been defeated. They are still alive, and they assert this life through their laughter.

The Scarperer is by no means a classic. Yet it is not merely a bit of froth—a humorous crime story. *The Scarperer* possesses a very relevant theme: man is a rather helpless, ridiculous creature who lives in a universe over which he has little control; those who think their best-laid plans are of much worth are fools. Just before Aunt Jeannie shouts "murderers" at the Scarperer and his crew, she is perusing a wall poster: "It showed a photograph of a cler-

gywoman, or a lady with a huge, pearly smile, orange lips and
platinum hair. The text was in English and read: 'American Cul-
tural Center of the Left Bank. Direct to Paris from West Chuzzle-
wit, Mass. The Rev. Mrs. Moore will deliver her famous lecture:
What Makes Things Happen'" (124)—"What Makes Things
Happen," indeed. In the world which Behan has created, blind
chance makes things happen. The Scarperer and his men are evil,
but they are unsuccessful not because they are evil, but because
they are unlucky. *The Scarperer* also asserts that in the world
which will ultimately reward all alike, it is better to enjoy life than
to waste time taking the lives of others.

II   Hold Your Hour and Have Another

Hold Your Hour and Have Another, published in 1963, is a collection of articles which Behan published in the *Irish Press* from
1954 to 1956. At the time the articles were being gathered for
collection, Behan was too ill to oversee the work so the task fell to
Rae Jeffs, who did a very competent job of selecting the best columns which Behan had written for inclusion in the book.

No excuses need be made for *Hold Your Hour and Have Another.* The articles which make up the book were designed for
light amusement. They fulfill this purpose admirably, and most of
them transcend topical and geographic boundaries. Crippen,
Maria Concepta, Mrs. Brennan, and Brending Behing, the people
of the book, sit in Dublin bars and speak almost solely of things
Irish; but the foibles and follies discussed are of universal interest.
Behan's articles are far above the normal journalistic fare, for
Hold Your Hour contains no columns of the parochial and topical
interest which constantly assail readers of Irish newspapers.
Moreover, all of the forty-six columns that make up *Hold Your
Hour* are written with a sure, workmanlike hand. Some of the
pieces are hilarious, evidencing the same sure sense of comic tim-
ing that is the hallmark of Behan's plays, and some exhibit an
almost Joycean fascination with language.

In "Overheard in a Bookshop," Behan describes the tribulations
of a lady assistant in a bookstore. She had gotten the job during
the Christmas rush, through the recommendation of the Labour
Department interviewer. Unfortunately, when the girl told the
Labour Department she had had three years experience in a
"cookshop," he thought she said "bookshop." When an old gentle-

man asks for a New Testament, she says, "Desperate sorry, I am, sir, but I am afraid it's not out yet. We have the old one of course, but I suppose you've read that" (14).[7] Some Americans ask the girl if she knows "Joyce is useless?" She replies that she does not care whether he was or not, "not knowing the man" (14). When another customer asks the clerk if she likes Kipling, she answers: "How could I know? When I never kippilled, and if I did it would be someone more me equals than you" (15).

"Dialogue on Literature" is a pub conversation in which the "budding genius Brending Behing" is put in his place by Crippen: "Never mind poor Brending Behing," said Crippen, "he doesn't know what he writes . . . Sad case . . . Only went to school half the time, when they were teaching the writing—can't read" (46). "The Hot Malt Man and the Bores" is not essentially concerned with either the Hot Malt Man or the Bores (Boers). The Bottle of Stout Man is the real center of attention, for his elaborate method of dodging his wife draws attention away from the Hot Malt Man's elaborate accounts of the Boer War. It seems that the pub which Behan describes in this column is sufficiently above street level for a passenger on the top floor of a double-decker bus to look directly into it. The Bottle of Stout Man's wife, who regularly rides on the top deck of the bus, looks through the pub window to see if her husband is inside. To escape surveillance, the Bottle of Stout Man, who knows the bus schedule to the moment, drops to the floor under a table. One such encounter Behan describes. The bus has just drawn up to the pub window and the Bottle of Stout Man has dropped to the floor:

The bus drew alongside the stop outside the pub and its top floor was on a dead level with the lounge in which we sat. The narrowness of the street made ourselves and the passengers intimate spectators of each other.

Only one of them took advantage of the proximity thus afforded: a hatched-faced oul' strap who swept the features of each of us with a searching sharpness and then, not altogether satisfied with what she'd seen, nodded grimly and almost threateningly as the bus bore her off. (64–65)

When Kinsella, one of the patrons of the bar, remarks that the woman who glared so fiercely at each of the assembled company was indeed ugly, the Bottle of Stout Man takes offense:

"Excuse yourself," said the Bottle of Stout man, "she is my wife, and I'll thank you to keep a civil tongue in your head." He spoke round at the company. "You can't expect a man to put up with remarks like that about the woman he loves."

Heads were nodded approvingly, and Kinsella was in some confusion.

"How was I to know she was your wife? And how did you know yourself it was her I was talking about? You were sitting on the floor and didn't see her."

"I recognized her from your description," said the Bottle of Stout man, with the quiet dignity of a trained mind. (64–65)

It naturally occurs to the other patrons of the pub to ask the Bottle of Stout Man why he doesn't go to another pub where his wife can't see him. Bottle of Stout replies: "You must forgive a sentimental old fool. . . . This is how we met. She looked in at me off the top of a tram. I'll never forget it" (66).

In "Trails of Havoc" the main event is the burial of a thumb. The assembled drinkers are celebrating the return of "Brending" from the "contingnent" by way of "Londing." Mrs. Brennan rises to the occasion with a story about a man who was sent to a surgeon for an operation on an ingrown toenail: "Me poor surjing read the card wrong and thought it was a head amputation was required. Amputated the head, God love him, very severe operating, the patient never come out of it and the poor surjing was disgraced for life" (127). Not to be outdone, Crippen contributes a story about the amputation and burial of a thumb. Apollo Swaine, "he got that name from hawking refreshments and shouting at the football matches, 'Cigarettes, chocolate, toffee-app-oll-oh' " (127), had a thumb amputated in the hospital. "Well, anyway, when he came out of the hospital he brought the thumb with him and gave a kind of a little wake for it in Jimmy-the-Sport's Bar up on our corner. Had it on the counter beside him, bringing it up to bury it. 'I'm going to put it where the rest of me will be when I die,' says Apollo. 'A fellow would look well on the last day, running round the Nevin [Glasnevin Cemetery] like a half-thick and asking everyone, and they gathering up their ould traps themselves, 'Ech, did you see e'er a sign of a thumb knocking round?' " (127). At Glasnevin Cemetery, above the sobs of the mourners, Apollo sings a proper song to the thumb, ending with the final line of "Danny Boy"—"And you will sleep in peace until I

come to thee." But, says Mrs. Brennan, "Still, it wasn't like having
a head amputating, having a tum amputating. When all is said
and done, a body does have two tums" (128).

Behan himself is the center of attention in "What are they at
With the Rotunda?" Here the young Brending claims to have
helped a relative out of a very serious situation indeed. The young
man is in need of help in running a musical review at the Torch
Theater. The Torch is not drawing a good house, for the compet-
ing houses—the Rotunda and the Star—are featuring singing
newsboys—the first, a mere singing newsboy; the second, a crippled singing newsboy. Behan's father, a sympathetic man where
relatives are concerned, suggests an attraction which will assure
that the Torch will have the best house of the three theaters: the
Torch should feature a "blind crippled singing newsboy." Fine,
says the relative, but where would one find such an attraction?

"I have him here," said your man, looking round.
I looked round, following his glance, but could see no newsboy,
blind, crippled, or any other sort.
"Where?" asks my old man.
"Here," says your man, putting his hand on my shoulder.
"Damn it," says the old man, "you wouldn't blind and cripple him
for the sake of a week's engagement? Different if you were doing the
grand tour of the thirty-two counties of Ireland and Newtownmount-
kennedy."

I wasn't blinded or crippled, but the next Monday night saw me on
the stage of the Torch, my few poor papers clutched to my side as I
leant on my crutch and gazed upon the sobbing multitude through
black glasses, balanced precariously on my one leg and my other
strapped up to the small of my back, singing the *Blind Ditty*. (136–37)

The whole of *Hold Your Hour and Have Another* is delightful
because it contains the occasional observations of a man who enjoyed both writing and people.

III "*Moving Out*" and "*A Garden Party*"

"Moving Out" and "A Garden Party" are two short radio plays
which Behan did for Radio Éireann in 1952.[8] When Micheal
O'hAodha, director of Radio Éireann, suggested that Behan try his
hand at matching the successful Irish radio serial, "The Foley
Family," these two short plays were Behan's contribution. As

O'hAodha says, "This series of two must constitute the shortest radio serial on record." [9] Later, when it was clear that the two were all that Behan was going to produce, Alan Simpson combined the two pieces and produced them at the Gate Theatre under the title *The New House*. Both plays are drawn from Behan's observations of his family. Neither is much good; in fact, the only value of these plays is that they indicate that Behan was a writer capable of a workmanlike performance. "Moving Out" deals with the move of the Hannigans (Behans) from Russell Street, where they have lived for some time, to the new housing project in Crumlin. Ma wants to move; Da does not. In a somewhat uncertain rendering of bitchy old Ma's outsmarting gruff old Da, Mrs. Hannigan finally gathers the family under her wing in that section of the city which she desires.

"A Garden Party" is a bit more clever. Mrs. Hannigan wants a garden. She has a load of manure delivered in the back yard to insure the garden's fertility. Her husband is not as malleable as the manure. He refuses to spade the garden. Under duress, however, he spreads a story that some stolen gold ornaments are buried in his garden. According to plan, the police dig up Jim Hannigan's garden for him.

IV Brendan Behan's Island

Brendan Behan's Island, published in 1962, is a three-part composite. Of the one hundred ninety-two pages of text, sixty-three are drawings by Paul Hogarth; thirty-two and one-half pages are taken up by work Behan had previously published; the remainder of the text consists of tape-recorded conversations which Behan had with Rae Jeffs. The book is imposingly bound and printed as if to disguise the fact that its contents, except for those pieces which Behan had previously published, are rather inconsequential. *Brendan Behan's Island* is not a book Behan had any reason to be proud of.

As originally conceived, *Brendan Behan's Island* was to be the same sort of book as John M. Synge's *The Aran Islands*. Behan's efforts, however, fell far short of Synge's. What was to have been a sort of geographical history of Ireland turns out to be a rambling and almost totally insignificant Behan monologue. The tape-recorded segments of *Brendan Behan's Island* are grouped under the general headings "Dublin's Fair City," "The Warm South,"

"The Bleak West," "The Black North." After reading Behan's remarks on these sections of his native land, one is, however, none the wiser concerning Ireland, its people, or Brendan Behan.

After Behan had completed the tapes and they had been edited, Rae Jeffs found to her dismay that Behan's rambling discourse could not be expanded to a sufficient number of pages to fill a respectable volume. Thus it was necessary to fill out the text with pieces Behan had previously published—two short stories, "A Woman of No Standing," and "A Confirmation Suit"; two mediocre poems (one on James Joyce, one on Oscar Wilde); and a short play, "The Big House."

"A Woman of No Standing" is a very short but very moving story about the death and funeral of a man who has been living apart from his family for many years. The "woman of no standing" is the woman with whom the man lived after he had left his wife and daughter. The story opens with the wife and daughter discussing the "woman of no standing" who insists on visiting the dying man even though she has no legal right to do so. The woman narrating the story is a friend of the wife and daughter of the dying man, but she has never seen the "other woman." When she does see her at the funeral, she is shocked. She sees not a painted lady in a fur coat, but "a poor middle-aged woman, bent in haggard prayer, dressed in the cast-off hat and coat of some flahool [generous] old one she's be doing a day's work for" (59).[10] When the narrator expresses her surprise to the wife, she replies: "Fur coat, how are you, and she out scrubbing halls for me dear departed this last four years—since he took bad" (59). The sympathy of the reader is finally and obviously with the "woman of no standing." Indeed, this woman has achieved a higher standing than Catholic law can grant. Her love may have been unrespectable, but it was passionate and true.

Both "A Confirmation Suit" and "A Woman of No Standing" are reminiscent of Joyce's *Dubliners*. Certainly, Behan possessed neither the raw genius nor the magnificent control of his material which Joyce had; but the epiphany, the moment of complete and thunderous revelation, is the focus in these two stories of Behan, as in all the stories in Joyce's *Dubliners*.

"A Confirmation Suit" is narrated by a twelve-year-old boy, obviously Behan. Miss McCann, a close friend of the young narrator's grandmother, has made a confirmation suit for the boy. Miss

McCann's normal stock in trade is shrouds, and the suit that she makes is so horribly "sissified" that, when the boy does wear it at confirmation and after, he wears it only briefly, and then he keeps it covered with his topcoat. Yet he hypocritically runs into Miss McCann's apartment from time to time, wearing the suit, to make her think that it is a favorite of his. The boy's mother decides to put a stop to his dishonesty: "She said I was a liar and a hypocrite, putting it on for a few minutes every week, and running into Miss McCann's and out again, letting her think I wore it every weekend. In a passionate temper my mother said she would show me up, and tell Miss McCann, and up like a shot with her, for my mother was always slim, and light on her feet as a feather, and in next door. When she came back she said nothing, but sat at the fire looking into it." (152).

The boy does not believe that his mother has indeed told Miss McCann, so he immediately rushes to the old woman's apartment to put on another show for her benefit. When he runs in the door, he sees her "bent over the sewing-machine and all I could see was the top of her old grey head, and the rest of her shaking with crying, and her arms folded under her head" (153). During the winter Miss McCann dies, and the boy does penance extreme for one so young: "At the funeral, I left my topcoat in the carriage and got out and walked in the spills of rain after her coffin. People said I would get my end, but I went on till we reached the graveside, and I stood in my Confirmation suit drenched to the skin. I thought this was the least I could do" (153). The moment of revelation, the moment of sympathetic communion is gracefully formed, and then revealed beautifully and without sentimentality.

"The Big House," a radio play first broadcast by the B.B.C. in 1957, was later a part of the program at the festival of Irish comedy at Stratford's Theatre Royal. The play is not very good, for it is crude without cleverness and formless without reason. The play is supposedly a roughly allegorical rendering of the sad state in which Ireland finds itself. The Big House (Ireland) is left to the devices of an estate manager by Ananias and Boadicea Baldcock (absentee landlords) who decide they would rather live in England than in Ireland. Immediately after the Baldcocks leave for England, the estate manager, Chuckles Genockey (oppressed Ireland) begins selling off the cattle, the paintings, and even the very doors of the manor house. Chuckles is helped by

Angel the Englishman (rapacious British mercantilism). After they have completed the looting of the estate, Chuckles and Angel host a wild house-cooling party to give themselves an alibi. The plan contains much talk about Chuckles' being justified in looting the estate since it was Cromwell who took it from the Irish in the seventeenth century. The talk and the characters who participate in it, however, are almost totally insignificant.

The play has no form. It is a series of vaguely connected anecdotes. The lewdness of the play is not clever and seems to be presented only for its own sake. The servant, Looney, for instance, tells of a Protestant minister and his wife who sometimes sleep in the Big House: "Himself and the wife, in that very bed. He's a protestant, of course, but a very religious man. The moans and groans of him there, kneeling on that very floor when he's saying his night prayers would go through you" (95). Granny Growl tells Granny Grunt that her husband was shot in the Dardanelles. Says Granny Grunt, sympathetically, "And a most painful part of the body to be shot" (108). When Granny Growl is asked to climb into the car for her ride to the house-cooling party, she says with a wee twinkle in her old eye, "At our age we enjoy a good ride. Its seldom that we get one" (109).

"The Big House" is not much of a play, but it possesses a vitality, a joy of life and language, which is absent in the tape-recorded segments of *Brendan Behan's Island.*

V Brendan Behan's New York

When time came for the publication of *Brendan Behan's Island,* Rae Jeffs discovered that the edited tapes of Behan's conversation were not sufficient to fill out a book; but, when *Brendan Behan's New York* was published in 1964, no one bothered with such mundane considerations. Only 70 of the 143 pages of *Brendan Behan's New York* are Behan's, and these pages come not from Behan's pen but from Rae Jeffs' tape recorder. The only good writing in the book is in the letters from Mary and Patrick Kearney. These letters, seemingly included as a sort of afterthought in the last pages of the book, report the soul-shattering experiences of nineteenth-century Irish immigrants in America.[11] The letters are only vaguely related to either Brendan Behan or New York, but they are compassionate and honest.

Behan's observations on New York are without sparkle or inspiration of any kind. The best thing that can be said about the book is that Behan probably realized that he was allowing his name to be used and that he was not even getting a very good price. Near the end of this sad book Behan gives those readers who are still with him a sort of release from their loyalty: "I will have forgotten this book long before you have paid your money for it, I can assure you. Singing your own songs or reading your own work, to me is a form of mental incest." [12] Before his last terribly sick years, Behan would not have demanded so little, either of himself or his audience.

VI   Confessions of an Irish Rebel

Confessions of an Irish Rebel, published in 1964 after Behan's death, was billed as a sequel to *Borstal Boy. Confessions,* however, is not worthy of being associated with *Borstal Boy.* Chronologically, it covers the time from Behan's release from Hollesley Bay until his marriage to Beatrice in 1955. Creatively, it contains hardly anything Behan could have been proud of. The book was the third of Behan's tape-recorded volumes; and, as was the case with *Brendan Behan's Island* and *Brendan Behan's New York,* the manuscript was edited into its final form by Rae Jeffs. Mrs. Jeffs undoubtedly did her best, but the tapes which Behan had made with her left her very little to work with. *Confessions of an Irish Rebel* is anecdotal, uninspired, and totally without literary merit. The best parts of the book, in fact, are lifted whole from *Borstal Boy.* Behan was a writer of wonderful talent and a talker of sparkling vitality, but *Confessions* shows him in neither of these roles.

Perhaps the best way to take *Confessions of an Irish Rebel* is to accept one of the incidents described in the narrative as a sort of metaphor for Behan's condition at the time he was taping the book. The incident has to do with one of Behan's earliest drinking experiences, when he could hardly have been more than seven or eight years old. With his indulgent and petting old grandmother, Brendan had set off to deliver the ailing Mrs. Murphy to the Hospice for the Dying. Mrs. Murphy insists, however, on stopping off for a "quick one" along the way, and the first drink she insists on having is not the last:

After having visited about seven public houses on the north side of Dublin, we proceeded to do a little drinking on the south side. We emerged from a public house opposite the Hospice for the Dying at eight o'clock in the evening, having left our native north-east at ten o'clock in the morning and I was twisted, as the saying has it, physically as well as in the other way; my head was sunk on my left shoulder.

In the spills of rain, an old gentleman came over to my grandmother. "That's a beautiful boy," he said, " 'Tis a pity he's deformed."

"The curse of Jaysus on you. That child is not deformed. He's just got a couple of drinks taken." [13]

Indeed, the deformities of *Confessions of an Irish Rebel* are directly attributable to alcohol.

CHAPTER 7

Summation

B EHAN can not be ranked among the great writers, for he did
not produce a sufficient volume of work, and even what he
did produce is not without flaw. Behan was not a Keats, an author
who produced a few nearly perfect works of art and then died
before his genius had fully developed. If Behan had lived longer
and written more, he probably would not have developed his art
or his vision much beyond that of the works which have made him
famous.

Nevertheless, Behan was much more than a gifted leprechaun.
He was a conscious artist, and the charge that his work is slapdash
is not altogether justified. He took the same liberties with traditional notions of language, plot construction, and character development as have many other contemporary writers. He realized,
with such writers as Beckett, Ionesco, Osborne, and Pinter, that
nineteenth-century standards would not serve twentieth-century
artists. Unfortunately, a good many critics who admire the unorthodox structure of the plays of Beckett or those of Pinter decry
the same structure in Behan's plays. *Waiting for Godot* has no
plot in the traditional sense. This, the critics say, is a component
of Beckett's art; but Behan's use of the same sort of plot is, quite
unjustifiably, frequently cited to prove his lack of talent.

Behan possessed a marvelous comic talent. That he wasted a
good deal of it cannot diminish his solid achievements. He wrote
two of the best plays of the contemporary theater, and one of the
best autobiographies of this century. He wrote with an exuberance and a humanity which will remain unexcelled. To a confused
and self-destructive world, Behan gave a simple and cogent re-
minder: human existence, though painful, is worthwhile. Or, as
Behan stated it in *The Quare Fellow,* life is "a bloody sight better
than death any day of the week."

Notes and References

Chapter One

1. Dominic Behan, *My Brother Brendan* (New York, 1965), pp. 158–59.
2. Rae Jeffs, *Brendan Behan: Man and Showman* (London, 1966), p. 251.
3. Ireland's Registry of Births, Marriages and Deaths contains no record of Behan's birth. The family, however, agrees on February 9, 1923.
4. Sean O'Tauama, ed., *Naubhéarsaíocht* (Dublin, 1950), pp. 106–107.
5. See Sean McCann, ed., *The World of Brendan Behan* (London, 1965), p. 187.
6. Brendan Behan, "Moving Out" and "A Garden Party," ed. Robert Hogan, *The Short Play Series, #3* (Dixon, California, 1967).
7. There are several Borstal institutions in England. They are the approximate equivalent of the United States reform schools.
8. Jhan and June Robbins, "Beatrice and Brendan Behan: Love Remembered," *Redbook* (March, 1966), p. 60.
9. Robbins, p. 104.
10. Robbins, p. 105.
11. Jeffs, p. 49.
12. Robbins, p. 108.
13. Collin MacInnes, "The Writings of Brendan Behan," *London Magazine* New Series (August, 1962), p. 53.
14. Jeffs, p. 66.
15. Malcolm Muggeridge, "Brendan Behan at Lime Grove," *New Statesman* (March 27, 1964), p. 488.
16. Seamus O'Kelley, "I Knew the Real Brendan Behan," *Irish Digest* (June, 1964), p. 69.
17. Alan Simpson, *Beckett and Behan and a Theatre in Dublin* (London 1962), pp. 51–52.
18. *Ibid.*, p. 53.
19. Alan Brien, "A Wreath for Brendan Behan," *Irish Digest* (May, 1964), p. 82.

20. Augustine Martin, "Brendan Behan," *Threshold*, XVIII (1963), p. 24.

21. Brian Behan, "Brendan," Spectator (July 17, 1964), p. 78.

22. Simpson, p. 30.

23. Dominic Behan, p. 25.

24. Brendan Behan, *Confessions of an Irish Rebel* (London, 1965; New York, 1965), p. 121, hereafter cited as *Confessions*. The London and New York publications of this book differ only slightly. All quotations from this text, unless specifically noted, are from the London edition.

25. George E. Wellwarth, *The Theater of Protest and Paradox: Developments in the Avante-Garde Drama* (New York, 1964), p. 258.

26. Robbins, p. 104.

27. *Ibid.*, p. 110.

28. Jeffs, p. 110.

29. Brian Behan, *With Breast Expanded* (London, 1964), p. 22.

30. Robbins, p. 110.

31. *The World of Brendan Behan*, p. 40.

32. Letter to the author from James Bourke, December 30, 1966.

33. Brian Behan, *Spectator*, p. 78.

34. *The World of Brendan Behan*, p. 23.

35. Sean O'Callaghan, *The Easter Lily: The Story of the I.R.A.* (London, 1956), p. 152. Certainly, as O'Callaghan says, the bombing campaign was ill-conceived to promote the cause the I.R.A. was fighting for:

The I.R.A. bombing campaign in England did more to alienate sympathy from the I.R.A. in England and Ireland than any other event in its chequered history. It was a campaign that invoked the hatred of the English people for Irishmen of every class and creed. Even those who were sympathetic to the Irish cause could have nothing but loathing for the men who originated this senseless campaign of terror and violence. It was a campaign which could have only one ending, the ruthless suppression of the I.R.A. in England and Ireland. It did much to instill bitterness against the I.R.A. in the de Valera Government, a bitterness which finally broke the power of the I.R.A. in 1941, with the death on hunger strike of Liam d'Arcy, the deaths by the hangman's noose of two men taken on a raid in Dublin in August 1940, and the execution by shooting of Sean McCaughy, Adjutant-General of the I.R.A. in 1941. (150).

An additional comment on the I.R.A. bombing campaign is that the cynical hand of Nazi Germany played a relatively important role. Had the Germans helped more materially, the I.R.A. might at least have been placed in the semi-respectable role of employing whatever weapons they found available, no matter how dubious those weapons. That the Germans ventured very little except immoral support makes the I.R.A. bombing campaign appear to be the action of a gullible and shallowly romantic group. A metaphor of the romantic ineffectuality of this episode in I.R.A. history can be seen in the fate of Sean Russell and Frank Ryan. Russell, Chief-of-Staff of the I.R.A., called "the old incorruptible" by his men, died of a ruptured duodenal ulcer on board a German submarine. Frank Ryan, his aide, who previously had led a small force of I.R.A. volunteers to fight in the Spanish Civil War, died in Germany before the end of the war. The dreams of Russell and Ryan were indeed noble, yet perhaps rather shallow, in that they paid only nominal attention to reality.

36. *The World of Brendan Behan*, p. 18.
37. Brendan Behan, *Borstal Boy* (New York, 1959), p. 3.
38. *Confessions*, pp. 31–32.
39. *The World of Brendan Behan*, p. 50.
40. *Ibid.*, p. 51.
41. *Confessions*, p. 93.
42. *Ibid.*, p. 95.
43. *Ibid.*, p. 96.
44. Eoin O'Mahoney, "A Memory of Brendan Behan," *Daily Egyptian* (April 27, 1966), p. 4.
45. *The World of Brendan Behan*, p. 67.
46. Dominic Behan, p. 47.
47. *Ibid.*, p. 156.
48. *Borstal Boy*, p. 94.
49. Simpson, p. 35.
50. *Envoy* (May, 1950).
51. Dominic Behan, p. 78.
52. Simpson, p. 38. For a full account of "The Catacombs" and its inhabitants see Simpson, pp. 34–38, and Anthony Butler's account in *The World of Brendan Behan*, pp. 141–44.
53. Simpson, p. 3.
54. Letter to the author from Jimmy Bourke, December 30, 1966. Mr. Bourke, who uses the pen name of Seamus de Burca, has written several well-known plays for the Irish theater.
55. Robbins, p. 104.
56. Brendan Behan, "A Tantalising Tale," *Fianna* (June, 1936), p. 30.
57. *Ibid.*
58. *Ibid.*
59. *Confessions*, p. 219.
60. *Borstal Boy*, p. 261.

61. *Ibid.*, p. 261.
62. *The World of Brendan Behan*, p. 70.
63. Jeffs, p. 31.
64. *Confessions*, p. 242.
65. *Times Literary Supplement* (November 24, 1966), p. 1104.
66. Jeffs, p. 41.
67. Brian Behan, *Spectator*, p. 79.

Chapter Two

1. *Confessions*, p. 31.
2. Sam Hynes, "An Irish Success," *Commonweal* (March, 1960), p. 628.
3. See Orville Prescott's review of *Borstal Boy, New York Times* (February 27, 1959), p. 23, which condemns Behan's use of profanity; Howard Taubman's review of *The Hostage, New York Times* (October 2, 1960), Sec. II, p. 1, which assumes that the wealth of comedy in the play removes it from the realm of art; and Stephen Ryan's review of *The Hostage, Catholic World* (November, 1960), pp. 126–27, which attacks Behan for "blasphemy," "perversion," and calls *The Hostage* a "sick" play.
4. Paul Lauter, ed., *Theories of Comedy* (Garden City, New York: 1964), p. xv.
5. Max Eastman, *Enjoyment of Laughter* (New York, 1936), p. 336.
6. William McCollom, "Form and Attitude in Comedy," *Drama Survey* (Spring–Summer, 1963), p. 47.
7. Aristotle, *Poetics*, chapters 1–9. Translation based on that by S. H. Butcher, Lauter, pp. 13–14. (The translation of this passage from Aristotle's *Poetics* and also the passage from Cicero's *De Oratore* was done by Lauter, who revised older translations for inclusion in his anthology.)
8. Cicero, "On the Character of the Orator," *De Oratore*, Book II. Translation based on that by George Barnes and J. S. Watson, Lauter, p. 24.
9. Donatus, "A Fragment on Comedy and Tragedy," translation by George Miltz specifically for this anthology. Lauter, p. 27.
10. Lucio Olimpio Giraldi, "Ragionamento in difesa di Terentio," trans. Bernard L. Weinberg, *History of Literary Criticism in the Italian Renaissance* (Chicago, 1961), p. 289.
11. Ben Jonson, "Dedicatory Epistle to Volpone," *The Works of Ben Jonson* (London, 1875), Vol. 3, p. 160.
12. Henri Bergson, *Laughter*, translated by Claudesley Bereton and Fred Rothwell (New York, 1912), p. 197.
13. James K. Feibelman, *Aesthetics* (New York, 1949), p. 139.

14. George Meredith, *An Essay on Comedy and the Uses of the Comic Spirit* (New York, 1956), p. 133.

15. George Santayana, "The Comic Mask," *Soliloquies in England* (New York, 1922), p. 137.

16. George Santayana, "Carnival," *Soliloquies in England* (New York, 1922), p. 191.

17. Susanne K. Langer, *Feeling and Form* (New York, 1953), p. 331.

18. *The Quare Fellow and The Hostage: Two Plays by Brendan Behan* (New York, 1964), Evergreen Black Cat Edition (Grove Press), p. 182.

19. Langer, pp. 340–41.

20. Eric Bentley, *The Life of the Drama* (New York, 1964), pp. 301–2.

21. Martin Esslin, *The Theatre of the Absurd* (New York, 1961), p. 292.

22. Robert Corrigan, "The Theatre in Search of a Fix," *Theatre in the Twentieth Century* (New York, 1963), p. 13.

Chapter Three

1. *The World of Brendan Behan,* p. 184.

2. Simpson, p. 6–8.

3. *Ibid.,* p. 52.

4. *The World of Brendan Behan,* p. 163–68.

5. Simpson, p. 55.

6. Judith Crist, Review of *The Quare Fellow, New York Herald Tribune,* November 28, 1958.

7. Brooks Atkinson, Review of *The Quare Fellow, New York Times* (November 29, 1958).

8. See review in *London Times* (October 5, 1961).

9. Ihan Hassan, *Radical Innocence: Studies in the Contemporary Novel* (Princeton, New Jersey; 1961), p. 116.

10. Elizabeth Hardwicke, "Word of Mouth," Review of *La Turista* by Sam Shephard, *New York Review of Books* (April 6, 1967), p. 8.

11. James L. Rosenberg, "Melodrama," *The Context and Craft of Drama,* ed. Robert W. Corrigan and James L. Rosenberg (San Francisco, 1964), p. 172.

12. *Ibid.,* pp. 177–78.

13. *Confessions,* p. 56.

14. Kenneth Tynan, Review of *The Quare Fellow, The Observer* (May 25, 1956).

15. John Russell Taylor, *Anger and After: A Guide to the New British Drama* (London, 1962), p. 105.

16. Vivian Mercier, *The Irish Comic Tradition* (Oxford, 1962), pp.

49–50. In this book, Mercier presents very persuasive evidence to prove his thesis: "Gaelic literature has from the earliest times shown a bent for wild humour, a delight in witty word play, and a tendency to regard satire as one of the indispensable functions of the literary man" (vii).

17. Crist, Review of *The Quare Fellow.*

18. Richard Hayes, "The Irish Presence," *Commonweal* (January, 1959), p. 438.

19. Page numbers in parentheses refer to quotations from the plays and, unless otherwise specified, are taken from *The Quare Fellow and The Hostage: Two Plays by Brendan Behan* (New York, 1964), Evergreen Black Cat Edition.

20. Taylor, p. 104.

Chapter Four

1. *The World of Brendan Behan,* p. 187.

2. Jeffs, p. 42.

3. *Ibid.,* p. 49.

4. Review of *The Hostage, London Times* (October 15, 1958), p. 89.

5. This and all subsequent New York newspaper reviews of the September 20, 1960, performance of *The Hostage* can be found in *New York Critics Theatre Reviews,* Vol. XXI, 28.

6. Esslin, p. 291.

7. *Ibid.,* p. 230.

8. Harold Clurman, Review of *The Hostage, Nation* (October 8, 1960), p. 236.

9. Benedict Kiely, "That Old Triangle: A Memory of Brendan Behan," *Hollins Critic* (February, 1965), p. 7.

10. Stephen Ryan, Review of *The Hostage, Catholic World* (November, 1960), p. 126.

Chapter Five

1. These typescripts are in the Irish Collection in the libraries of Southern Illinois University, Carbondale, Illinois.

2. C. A. Joyce, who was governor when Behan was interned at the Feltham Boys Prison, read part of the typescript of *Borstal Boy* and agrees that "the uncensored version was much more hilarious and outrageously funny than the final product." Joyce, however, says that the "cleaning up process" did not hurt the book much. This assertion seems as unlikely as the one which Joyce makes declaring that Behan did not use four-letter-words in prison. *The World of Brendan Behan,* pp. 61–62.

3. TS and *Points* version, "Bridewell Revisited."

4. Numbers in parentheses refer to pages in *Borstal Boy* (New York, 1959).

5. TS and *Points* version, "Bridewell Revisited."

6. Michael Campbell, "Book and Author," *Irish Times* (October 25, 1958), p. 6.

7. Potatoes.

8. Martin Sheridan, Review of *Borstal Boy, Irish Times* (October 25, 1958).

9. Orville Prescott, Review of *Borstal Boy, New York Times* (February 27, 1959).

10. John Wain, Review of *Borstal Boy, New York Times Book Review* (February 22, 1959).

11. J. D. Salinger, *The Catcher in the Rye* (New York, 1959), Modern Library Edition, p. 17.

Chapter Six

1. Rae Jeffs, Afterword to *The Scarperer* (New York, 1964).

2. Emile Capouya, "Gift of Gab on the Lam," *Saturday Review* (June 20, 1964), p. 36.

3. *Times Literary Supplement* (November 23, 1966), p. 1104.

4. Anne O'Neill Barna, Review of *The Scarperer, New York Times Book Review* (June 24, 1964), p. 5.

5. Review of *The Scarperer, Prairie Schooner,* XXXIX, 2 (Summer, 1965), p. 175.

6. Numbers in parentheses refer to pages in *The Scarperer* (New York, 1964).

7. Numbers in parentheses refer to pages in Brendan Behan's *Hold Your Hour and Have Another* (New York, 1963).

8. The plays were published in 1967 by Robert Hogan's Proscenium Press (Dixon, California).

9. Micheal O'hAodha, Introduction to "Moving Out" and "A Garden Party."

10. Numbers in parentheses refer to pages in *Brendan Behan's Island* (New York, 1962).

11. The letters are reproduced from Seamus de Burca's *The Soldier's Song* (Dublin, 1957).

12. *Brendan Behan's New York,* p. 115.

13. *Confessions,* p. 109.

Selected Bibliography

PRIMARY SOURCES

"The Big House." *Evergreen Review*. vol. V, 20, (September–October, 1961), 40–63.

Borstal Boy. London: Hutchison and Co., 1958. New York: Alfred Knopf, 1959.

Brendan Behan's Island: An Irish Sketchbook. London: Hutchison and Co., 1962. Tape-recorded conversations. The text is filled out with drawings by Paul Hogarth and several short pieces which Behan had previously published.

Brendan Behan's New York. New York: Bernard Geis Associates, 1964. More tape-recorded conversations. Drawings by Paul Hogarth.

Confessions of an Irish Rebel. London: Hutchison and Co., 1965. New York: Bernard Geis Associates, 1965.

Hold Your Hour and Have Another. London: Hutchison and Co., 1963. A collection of the best columns which Behan wrote for the *Irish Press*, 1954–1956. Drawings by Beatrice Behan. Boston: Little, Brown, 1964.

The Hostage. London: Methuen and Co., 1958. New York: Grove Press, 1959.

"Moving Out" and *"A Garden Party."* Ed. Robert Hogan, Dixon, California: Proscenium Press, 1967. Two short plays based on the happenings of the Behan household.

The Quare Fellow. London: Methuen and Co., 1956. New York: Grove Press, 1957.

The Quare Fellow and The Hostage. New York: Grove Press, 1964.

The Scarperer. Garden City, New York: Doubleday and Co., 1964. The book form of the serial which Behan wrote for the *Irish Times* in 1953.

SECONDARY SOURCES

BEHAN, BRIAN. "Brendan," *The Spectator*, July 17, 1964, pp. 77–79. Sensitive, understanding sketch of brother Brendan.

BEHAN, DOMINIC. *My Brother Brendan*. London: Leslie Frewin, 1965. Contains some interesting and revealing anecdotes, but Dominic is clearly more interested in revealing his own activities than those of his brother Brendan.

DE BURCA, SEAMUS. "The Essential Brendan Behan," *Modern Drama*, VII (1966), 374–81. A quiet reminiscence by one of Behan's favorite relatives. Burca knew a Behan which the sensational accounts of journalists never revealed: "He was a lovely gentle soul. He loved the poor and he loved old people. He was the happiest of all singing his ballads in the company of old women and old men. Peace be to his soul."

CAULFIELD, MAX. "A Portrait of Brendan Behan Drinking Life's Last Bitter Dregs," *Fact*, III (January–February, 1966), 18–25. An account of Behan shortly before his death; at this time Behan was too sick to control either his mind or body.

DUPREY, RICHARD. "The Bloodshot World of Brendan Behan," *The Critic*, XX (December, 1961–January, 1962), 55–57. Says Duprey, who admires Behan in spite of himself, "The most disturbing thing about the Rabelaisian denunciations of Brendan Behan as he squints at us through bloodshot eye, is that much of what he says is true."

ESSLIN, MARTIN. *The Theatre of the Absurd.* Garden City, New York: Doubleday, 1961. Classic work, notable for both breadth and depth. Behan is not discussed, but Esslin's chapters on "The Tradition of the Absurd" and "The Importance of the Absurd" are especially relevant to Behan.

JEFFS, RAE. *Brendan Behan, Man and Showman.* London: Hutchison, 1966. The pleasure and pain of Behan's company detailed by the editor of the tape-recorded books. Covers the period 1957 to Behan's death.

KIELEY, BENEDICT. "That Old Triangle: A Memory of Brendan Behan," *The Hollins Critic*, II (February, 1965). The best single article written on Behan. Kiely is a rarity, an Irishman who is not jealous of Behan. His view is balanced and perceptive: "He was brave from boyhood to death, but there were no false heroics about him, and he felt that between mangling and martyrdom there should be some satisfactory poetic, and preferably unpainful relationship."

MCCANN, SEAN, ed. *The World of Brendan Behan.* London: New English Library, 1965. New York: Twayne Publishers, 1966. Essays and reminiscences by diverse hands. The picture of Behan which emerges from this book is remarkably full and remarkably fair.

MACINNES, COLIN. "The Writings of Brendan Behan," *London Magazine*, II (August, 1952), 53–61. MacInnes was one of the first to treat Behan seriously as a writer. MacInnes' article does an excellent job of proving his thesis that Behan is an artist with an essentially tragic view of life.

MERCIER, VIVIAN. *The Irish Comic Tradition.* London: Oxford Press, 1962. Excellent analysis of Irish comedy. Behan's comedy is not analyzed, but he clearly fits into the Irish comic pattern.

ROBBINS, JHAN and JUNE. "Beatrice and Brendan Behan: Love Remembered," *Redbook* (March, 1966), pp. 60–63ff.

SIMPSON, ALAN. *Beckett and Behan and a Theatre in Dublin.* London: Routledge and Kegan Paul, 1962. A strangely neglected book, for what Simpson has to say about Beckett and Behan is much more piercing and relevant than much of the later scholarly writing on these two authors.

TAYLOR, JOHN RUSSELL. *Anger and After: A Guide to the New British Drama.* London: Methuen and Co., 1962. An excellent general survey of recent British theater, though the number of authors Russell includes necessarily restricts the depth of his analyses. The chapter on Behan is no exception.

WELLWARTH, GEORGE. *The Theatre of Protest and Paradox: Developments in the Avante-Garde Drama.* New York: New York University Press, 1964. The same sort of survey as *Anger and After,* though Continental and American drama is included. Wellwarth's book is inclusive, as is Russell's; it also resembles Russell's in that it contains little criticism of any depth.

Index